The Last Dead Soldier Left Alive

Aug 07

Dan

Peace,

R. B

The Last Dead Soldier Left Alive

Richard Boes
P.F.C.
RA11766968

iUniverse, Inc.
New York Lincoln Shanghai

The Last Dead Soldier Left Alive

iUniverse books may be ordered through booksellers or by contacting:

iUniverse
2021 Pine Lake Road, Suite 100
Lincoln, NE 68512
www.iuniverse.com
1-800-Authors (1-800-288-4677)

ISBN-13: 978-0-595-41858-9 (pbk)
ISBN-13: 978-0-595-86204-7 (ebk)
ISBN-10: 0-595-41858-9 (pbk)
ISBN-10: 0-595-86204-7 (ebk)

Printed in the United States of America

Contents

Acknowledgments

I would like to thank Janet Steen, William and Natalie Boes, James McGrath, Barbara Klar, Tom DiCillo, Kim Wozencraft, Norm Green, Margaret Gormley, Luc Sante, Janet Hahne Hofsted, and Richard Harper, *thank you.*

You're not gonna believe this, but it's the fucking truth. More than 58,000 Americans died for nothing in Vietnam. Since the war, it's estimated (depending upon the source) that some 20,000, or as many as 200,000 Vietnam veterans, would-be survivors, have committed suicide. And all for nothin'! Yeah, something's terribly wrong. Me, you, the fuckin' government. I do, I do believe we were all wrong.

◆　　◆　　◆

… In memory of 58,219, countless others, and how many more? …

1

"My Blue Block of Wood"

It was a plane full of strangers, a hundred, a hundred and fifty of us maybe, but no one I remembered or seemed to know from a year ago. Just this deafening silence like the kind that stops you at the moment somethin' or someone dies. Jesus, it ain't me anymore reflected in the window glass but ghosts, faces I'd known, Buttkins, Henderson, Walsh, Casey fuckin' Jones. A backdrop of flares, tracer bullets, an explosion here and there like fireworks across a black screen, a black sky, a black hole we were shooting out of as we taxied down the runway.

Even in this pressured cabin the heat still clung to my flesh, the stench, the taste of burnt rotting corpses still permeated the air. You couldn't wash it off, there hadn't been time, no debriefing, besides it was stuck in my throat, suspended somehow between home and my gut.

We were all in jungle fatigues, worn and faded green, muddy, some ripped, others blood stained. As was the practice, I'd crossed off days on a pocket calendar, sealed tight in a personalized, plastic, First Cav, waterproof wallet. Still the ink bled, but eventually I called myself, "Short!"

"Short! Three days and a wake up," Brown yelped. Now, this here was the fuckin' wake up, I was in tow, goin' back to the world. Thinking, couldn't stop myself, all the things I'd truly missed, all the things I'd do. Still, I sat in disbelief, why me?

I couldn't stop my legs from moving, up and down, side to side, in and out of time. There was a chorus stirring about me, a rustling movement goin' nowhere. That final fear resonated in everyone's eyes, what if we take a fucking rocket? What if we crash? After all this shit, the irony, Jesus, wouldn't it be my luck. I continued my search back and forth, front to back as if scanning a perimeter, a fuckin' tree line. It wasn't the enemy I was looking for, not this time, but someone, anyone I might recognize. No one it seemed. We'd all been abandoned by a meaningless war, forsaken on all fronts, both sides, both for and against. Even to ourselves we were strangers. God was absent. I was alone.

A tour of duty was a year, troops coming and going every day like a factory march. Dispersed, replaced, gathered up, and sent off. This was very much an individual war. I'd left everyone in my platoon, my company behind as others had previously left me. I wasn't supposed to care. I didn't! When Myles left a few months earlier, he cried and held me in his arms. He was drunk. O'Brien borrowed ten bucks he was gonna mail to me, but six days back in the world he deliberately drove off a bridge in his brand-new red Corvette. And Casey, Casey re-upped for the fuckin' dope. This war was about getting me out alive, and up to now I'd been victorious.

The pilot broke silence announcing over the p.a., "Gentleman, we've just cleared Vietnam airspace." We all cheered, but it was like someone trying to laugh who can't stop crying, like trying to make small talk at your best friend's funeral. Quickly the silence returned. I couldn't stop my legs from pumping. There in the glass were only shadows of who I once was, who I didn't recognize anymore, a fuckin' ghost.

I do, I do believe, I do. Smacking my knees together, these muddy boots like ruby red slippers. It's over. I'm going, "I'm goin' home."

We stopped twice briefly to refuel, once in Thailand, then Hawaii, and eighteen hours later landed in California. We were bused to a military base. No wire mesh on the windows anymore to expel explosive cocktails, no fires in the skies like when I got to the war. No heat, no stench clinging to my flesh, but this one, this taste I'd brought home in my mouth like the promise of milk and honey gone sour. There wasn't any fanfare, there was no one. We walked through a barn door, the back door of a building, a basement entrance, down a long corridor of bare bulbs and concrete, what looked like a warehouse, a slaughterhouse or even a fuckin' prison like I was gonna be interrogated, tortured, or somethin', somethin' bad. And over the archway was a sign that read, "Your Country's Proud of You."

"Fuck you!" shouted someone. Others laughed, or tried to.

"The joke's on us," I told the guy to my right, who tossed up a middle finger. Some officer in clean starched khakis, donning a blonde butch stuck-up haircut, broke us down in columns and pointed us in which direction to go.

"Welcome home, welcome home, welcome home," he whispered as we passed in rows of two. No one saluted, and I could tell we made him nervous.

Welcome home motherfucker! was my only thought, pretended to trip and bumped him up against the wall. "Excuse me, Sir."

I took a shower, a fuckin' hot shower and got me a change of clothes. Goddamn dress greens! I wasn't thrilled about having to wear a uniform. Besides the stories of being spit upon and the name calling, a rumor was circulating that a woman approached a soldier in a commercial airport, identified the patch on his arm as being the same as her son's, same as mine, he'd been killed. She wailed, "Why are you still alive?" Pulled a gun from her purse and shot him dead.

Some spiffy soldier, a fuckin' paper shuffler, sat behind a desk and asked if we had any wounds he needed to make note of. "Speak now, or forget about it." His name tag read "Pilot," all the hair he'd left on his head like cotton balls was in his ears. God was here, alive, and laughing. "I'm fine," I told him, ignoring the shrapnel that was still in my leg. "I just wanna go home." There was a free steak dinner, but no one I knew of was hungry for food. I collected my things, and soon enough was on a plane back east, and homeward bound.

◆   ◆   ◆

It was sometime after midnight and the airport was practically empty. In a day's time, I'd traveled from the hellish jungles of war and was just a forty-five minute car ride from home. I'd called Jimmy, my best friend since childhood, and he was en route. My family expected me sometime during the month, but had no idea I was soon to arrive. It felt strange wearing dress greens and not jungle fatigues, bright ribbons and patches instead of camouflage. These new shoes only hurt my feet, I missed my muddy boots. Still, I couldn't sit still and wait, but had to walk around.

All the shops were closed. I was too young for the bar, too young to vote, too young for anything, but not to die. So few people it seemed, and those who did pass avoided eye contact. I wanted so badly to celebrate, to yell out as fucking loud as I could get, I'm home! To grab some girl and dance about, dance the fuckin' skies like angels on occasion sometimes do, to sweep her off her feet with a passionate kiss. Like that photograph, that other war, a war that meant somethin', but no one seemed to notice me, no one cared. I was fuckin' invisible. I didn't fit. I didn't belong here. I might even welcome someone calling me a bad name, at least I'd be alive. Me, the keeper of a lost war, a war no one seemed to recognize, or desired any knowledge of. Jesus, it's all that

I'm about anymore. And if I could I'd fuckin' disappear like you wish I would. "If!" If only I could. And the enemy was silent, and the silence was killing me.

I tried saying something to someone, anyone, say anything like, what time is it? Nice weather we're having. Have you change for a dollar? Excuse me, Miss, my name is Lazarus, I'm back from the dead, and I ain't got a fuckin' clue.

This underwear I hadn't worn for a year, buttoned-up collar and tie, irritated the jungle rot, the pimpled sores that oozed in a straight line from the base of my neck to the balls of my crotch. There's too much starch in this shirt. I itched like a fuckin' leper on parade, a bad case of mistaken identity, and, and I had to pee. Where's the men's room? I could ask, but fuck it. I'd find it myself.

I lost the tie and unbuttoned a few buttons down my shirt, took the bayonet strapped to my leg and cut my underwear off. The bathroom was empty, so I thought, standing at the urinal having a good scratch, taking a leak, caught unawares as the janitor came out from the toilet area and dropped a large trash drum to the floor. "Incoming!"

Shrapnel flies up and out, hot and screaming, so the lower you get the better your chances. In a split second's nosedive, I was flat against the earth sucking up warm wet tile in a puddle of my own piss. A moment's flash and I'm back there, had I ever left? Where the fuck am I now?

"Sorry boy, you's okay?" A soft, black, gray whiskered face was leaning over me.

"Yeah," I said, "guess so," feeling only grateful it wasn't a rocket. He handed me a towel from around his neck.

"Dry's yourself," he winked with a surprising sky blue glass eye, scratched with fat nervous fingers atop his thinning hair. "Sold, it's the first four letters of soldier, a four letter word," he laughed, a disheartened-like punch-drunk fighter's wheeze. "And your sellin' price," shooin' a fly from his face, "wasn't even our freedom. My name's Elijah," he took up his mop. "There's no good wars to speak about, but at least my's generation, our war had a purpose."

"Thanks," I said as he took back his towel, and shook my hand.

"Wars is fought by us poor folk, us soldiers, is niggers, and all niggers is trained to die." He itched with a flurry of pokes at his nose. "Don't you let them make it your fault. You's hear me boy?" I just nodded my head and made my way for the exit. Elijah fumbled twice, dropped his mop to the floor. I wanted to catch it, but was too far off, too slow, too late. He called out as the door closed between us. "You's be a survivor!"

Me and Jimmy were both more than tired. He was against the war, an accountant now, not much for words. I didn't know what to say, or how to say it. We talked sports some, the Mets had won the World Series, the Jets the Super Bowl, the Knicks were NBA champs. Other than him reading every street sign, billboard, storefront we passed, we were mostly quiet. "Shop Rite," "Two Guys," "Kool, come up, all the way up." Yeah, I was feeling anxious, afraid, guilty I think about coming home.

Elijah was right. It wasn't my fault, it wasn't up to me. I didn't choose to be here, who would die, and who would come back. And there ain't no more Stockwell, Abrams, Smyth or Donny Gains. Jesus, and Rodney Brown who stood where I stood just moments before. "Short! Three days and a wake up," he yelped in a black man's drawl. "I's goin' back to the world! I's one lucky motherfucker!" And Betty, bouncin' Betty, she's a Goddamn landmine, bounced up in his lap, cut 'im in fuckin' two! And a B-40 rocket swallowed what was left into tiny little fucking pieces.

"Don't mean nothin'!" Myles said.

And I'll never know by just how much I missed her. Half a step maybe, "If!" Guess I'm one, one lucky motherfucker! Just these shards, bits of metal in my leg. And one, Rodney's one patch of black hair sunken in behind one eye swimming in a sea of brain matter, all pink, and blue, and gray. We collected 'im in a black bag, "I'm in pieces, bits and pieces!" Me and Myles kept singing, stomped our feet, scattered the fucking bits that weren't pieces anymore.

You're really alone during a rocket attack, there's nothin' anyone can do. You're really fuckin' alone, when the other guy's dead. "If!" As if he'd taken my place. And if you're one of the lucky ones you get to do it again. And again. And the repetition, over, over and again. And the pieces that won't fit together again like Humpty Dumpty didn't have to pick himself up. And all the King's horses wear blinders, and all the King's men believe their own lies. "Don't mean nothin'!" And the fucking fear that resonates, echoes back and forth, gnaws and eats away at you, over, over and again. It's worse than death. I do believe, I don't believe you! And who's the lucky motherfucker?

We sat at the tracks waiting for the train to pass. Its whistle and pulsing bark put me on edge, my feet on fuckin' trampolines. Here I was alone again, with Jimmy in the driver's seat, still waiting. I tried counting cars, seven, seventeen, seventy-eight, how many more before I'm home safe? The face in the windshield was Rodney's. All I really wanted was to be held, for someone to hold me.

Me and Jimmy met some twelve years ago, he was a few years older and my family'd just moved into the neighborhood. I had this old beat-up glove that was my Dad's and a blue block of wood I was using for a ball. I was throwing it high up against the side brick of the house and making basket catches like Willie Mays. The whole game was alive in my head, both teams, a miss was a run and it was one-one, in the bottom of the sixteenth. Jimmy approached unnoticed until he sneezed, a giant fuckin' sneeze. He was a tall skinny kid with a face like Goofy, a dried mop of brown hair, and a big long tweaked nose. I'd made a bad throw, and just missed catching it with a diving attempt into the bushes. "Nice try," he said, and goofed up a laugh like a jackass hee-haws. "That's it, game's over, you lose!" Jimmy invited me to join him and his friends up the block, the Dick Street Bombers. They had a real ball, and needed a center fielder.

In a few weeks time I was to be the best man at Jimmy's wedding. Sure we were happy to see each other, but something was missing, it just wasn't the same. Yeah, guess it was me who'd changed. I wanted to tell him about the war, about Rodney, what I'd seen and done, but didn't know how, couldn't find the words. Anyway, I didn't think he'd understand.

We were just a few miles from home and I had to say somethin', flush this spin cycle circlin' my brain, break my fuckin' silence. I mentioned meeting Elijah, him helping me up off the floor, and the conversation that followed. Suddenly and without warning, Jimmy's Mustang jumped the curb. He'd fallen asleep on me, and we were headed straight on for a telephone pole. The second thu-thump of the back tires woke him the fuck up. "Jesus!" he shrieked, but was slow to react. In one sweeping motion I reached over and cut the wheel to the left landing us back on the street. Jim was a bit shaken up, squeezed tight. "Sorry," he said, "coulda killed us."

"Don't mean nothin'!" I told 'im, and for a moment I was baggin' Rodney again. "Just stay awake, Jim. We're almost home." I never called him Jim. Something felt good inside, this wasn't like a rocket attack, there was more I could do than just be a passenger.

"See ya man, thanks for the ride." I closed the car door, Jimmy drove off. The house was all dark, no porch light left burning. Bones, my dog must of come home, but there ain't no barkin'. I climbed the steps, hit all the fuckin' cracks down the walk, another flight of steps. They never locked the front door, but something stopped me from opening it. I turned myself around, gazing up at the streetlight. A pair of my old sneakers still hung by their laces over telephone wire, deep blue shadow sifted through naked tree branches like distant fingers, reaching into, grabbing at a big thick slice of mud pitched black heavenly pie. No stars. Still no Bones.

Mom, Dad, my two younger brothers and sisters were inside sleeping. I felt this knot in my stomach like the whole fucking war was twisting up inside me, might I just fuckin' implode! I wouldn't wake them, I'd go quietly upstairs and go to bed. I'd see them come mornin'. I opened the screen door, stopped, and had to close it, opened and closed it again. Walked round the side of the house, doubled over, body doubled up, holdin' my stomach, leaned into some bushes and started throwing up. Once, twice, over and again until there was nothin', nothin' but bile, yellow sauce, until all I'd left me was less than empty, inside out. And there, right the fuck before my eyes, peering out at me, out from under dead leaves and a fresh spray of vomit was my blue block of wood. I scooped it up as if I'd found lost treasure, gold and silver bullion, and cleaned it off with a few swipes against the grass. I clenched it in my fist, couldn't help but smile. Bones came running up, his blackness all aglow, excited like welcoming me home.

I looked in for a moment at my youngest brother Billy, my godchild sleeping peacefully. As a child I was a sound sleeper. I once fell off the top bunk of a bunk bed and didn't wake up. Hearing the thud, my parents came rushing in from the living room and found me sleeping on the floor. Now I had to put my mattress on the floor, and it was a good thing that my room was the smallest in the house, most like a bunker, less of a target, it provided a false sense of security. Accustomed as I was to the constant barrage of noise a war makes, now the silent night of suburbia was keeping me awake.

After only a few weeks in Vietnam I knew every sound of darkness like a blind man knows his own home. What was incoming, cause for alarm, and what was going out. I slept on a thin dime, and the faint whistle of a distant rocket would call me out from a crowded dream. I'd be hugging mother earth like a babe for milk, sucking up mud like wanting breath, steel pot and flak jacket on. I'd have a fuckin' cigarette lit before the first round hit, before any siren ever sounded. "If!" And if it let up long enough you ran for a bunker.

I came to know with acute precision like a fine-tuned instrument, the difference, the distinction in every sound the blackness made. What were rockets, mortars, short rounds, a.k.a. friendly fire, s.n.a.f.u.! Fred took one in the shower. Small arms, M-60's, 79's, quad 50's, B-52's, and oh how the ground shook. Flares, claymores, bounce, fuckin' bouncin' Betty, fuck! Fuckin' B-40! "If!" A sapper left a satchel charge in a hooch two doors down. Don't mean nothin'! A luring Loach, whoop, whoop, whoop, draws out enemy fire, a seething Cobra and other gunships closin' in. Woof! Napalm jet streamers, and Puff, Puff the Magic Dragon, whose mini guns from on high could infiltrate every fuckin' square inch of space the size of a football field in a matter of seconds. Every twenty-seventh round was a tracer, and we watched cheering atop a bunker as the red whip, the red whip waved on, and on, and fuckin' on like hells bells rainin' down.

We were the supreme, ultimate firepower of the skies. Absolute, all-powerful, like God I thought like God lacks humility. But the enemy was underground, tunneled in beneath the earth, at the core of believing, beyond extinction.

Now I scanned about my room by the gray blue shadows of moon, and filtering streetlight, beads like tears patterned upon embroidered curtain lace. In the wake of the battle, tired enough, but unable to sleep. The rug was sky blue and grape juice stained, the walls needed more than paint. Jesus was missing limbs on the crucifix above, at the back of my brain, broken off by a touchdown pass that should have been caught. Dust collectors on bookshelves posing as trophies, old posters, banners, signed baseballs and other sports memorabilia. My bruised blue block of wood I'd placed on the dresser, my bayonet sheathed, asleep under my pillow. That picture, without any glass, a gentle boy laidback on a hillside, all blue jeans, white buttoned-down shirt, red vested, black shiny curls, an arm up shielding his eyes from the sun. Tell me, tell me again, please tell me your dreams?

That football is the precursor of war, the training fields, the same language. Kill, kill, kill! War is the ultimate sport, the culmination of sport. Kill, or be killed! Kill the Giants, Jets, Patriots, and Eagles. Kill the fuckin' Yankees, Braves, and Angels. Kill Babe Ruth! Killroy, he's not here anymore. Kill Jim Brown, John Brown, Charlie Brown, and Rodney Brown. "I's one lucky motherfucker!" Kill the fuckin' Gooks! Kill the Japs, the Krauts, the Commies, and the Jews. Kill Goliath! John the Baptist, John the Catholic, his brother Bobby, and Martin Luther nigger King Jr.!

"My God, My God, why hast Thou forsaken me?" Kill Jesus! And like Cain slew Abel, I am the plowman, the keeper of bad uprooted seedling, maimed and forged to wander. And Abraham, what of Isaac? Kill me!

Bones rests his head on my belly, looks me up, gives me a stare like what the fuck man, like he knows my thoughts like he feels bad for me because I'm a fuckin' nut job! "Good old Bones."

It's raining now, a somewhat soothing rain, rap, a pat, tap, and the occasional swish of a passing motorist endeavors to coddle me to sleep. It's not that hard monsoon rain that blinds the sky, or the sound of hot screaming metal cavorting off tin roofs, that piercing screech that howls and rips through tent canvas embedding itself below the heart at gut level.

Uncle Ho's birthday, I couldn't stop the thoughts. We were hit five times during the night with over ninety rockets. Every time I'd fall asleep. Again, over and again. We got no fuckin' sleep. From side to side, closer, overhead, then passing. Back and forth like walking giants. Giant steps. Explosive, deafening! Fe, fi, fo, fum! "If!" If one hits the roof you're dead! Away, and back again. Approaching, closer, fi, fo, fum! "If!" If one hits the roof, and again! Over and again like the buttoning and unbuttoning of shirts until all the buttons fall off.

I'd promised God I'd go to church every Sunday for the rest of my life. "If!" If he'd just get me the fuck outta here alive. The hooch in front of us was hit, and all twelve guys obliterated. The tent to the right, the one behind were all gone now. And still came the giants. Fi, fo, fum! And Casey, Casey took one in the shithouse while shootin' up at the war. Happy fuckin' trails! Swishhhhhh.

My eyes pop open, toothpick wide! This ain't no fuckin' war, this is my room, there's Bones asleep on the floor like old paint. Please, dear God, but for thy grace, grant us some fuckin' sleep. Rap, a pat, tap. Fe, fi, fo, there are no giants anymore. Swishhhhhh.

We sat on empty ammo boxes under a sweltering sky in twelve rows of five. It was Palm Sunday, my first Sunday in Vietnam and the last time I attended Mass. A Major, a priest who resembled Elijah, stood before us in bloody, torn jungle fatigues and addressed us as a group. The blood was blue. "I haven't time to hear your confessions, so just think of your sins, and you's forgiven." He made the sign of the cross pendulating his rifle muzzle through the air. I hadn't sinned yet, my uniform was clean. I was nothin', an F.N.G., a fuckin' new guy. What the fuck did I know? Was this ammo box really empty?

"If!"

The Major's face commenced to shed, and words fell off in drools of blue spittle, his flesh peeled back on sheets of wind and fell like raindrops into pools of blue blood. Everyone was going blue, bleeding, and crying blue tears. My arms, my hands, my fingers like tree branches sprouting blue streams. The Major's hair in one fell swoop burst into bright orange flame, arcing out across an orange sky, so orange as if a sunset had swallowed it whole. I put my hand to my face and my nose came back in my hand, blue lips impressed upon a blue palm. In a swishhhhh of orange blue vapor, the Major, Elijah priest was all gone.

I could feel my ears dribble, dripping off, my eyes leaking out of socket, waist deep in a whirl of blue bubble and torrent I was thrashed and spun about. From the heavens came a blue rain, rap, a pat, tap, and blue stoned hail the likes of hot screaming metal chunks, fi, fo, fum! A murderous raging pain in my chest gashed forth, bone pierced flesh like the great sea had been parted, and split me in fucking two. "My God," I cried out in slumberous garble. "Take all of me!"

Slam, "Fuck!" Into the wall, I'd kicked the dog. Smack! Against the window pane, cast down like a bad, scorned, forlorn angel into the bottom of the dresser, and out across the fuckin' floor. Low crawl, belly drag. I'm fuckin' belly up here now. Awake! Cold with sweat, naked, free, freezing. I'd bruised my head, my fist and rug burns to my knees and chest. My side hurts, and the curtain is torn. It's raining harder now, and the sky splits, flash, spits, rat, a tat, tat like machine gunfire. Kerplunk, plunkety, plunk into buckets, drain pipes like blood gutters, bullet holes, buttonholes, and this empty hollow feeling at the pit. I'd been pitted, gutless, so fucking vacant. Whose sins are these? Are we all really dead? What the fuck did Elijah want? And the moon's a grayish hint of blue hue, and shadows by streetlight upon the rain beaded window-glass silhouette the wall in black tears. Jesus, where's my blanket? Afraid to sleep anymore, but I need so badly, so bad to get warm.

◆   ◆   ◆

Three days back in the world and I'm up before the birds, before the trees, before the sky and branches reaching. Waiting, waiting for the sun to begin, for the heat to come up before I come out from my blanket. A train whistle off in the distance, up the block, two clicks. It ain't that kind of whistle or siren, and the fuckin' streetlight goes out. Again I'm in blue gray shadow, still waiting. Church bells, and the wind chimes off the back deck. Newsprint hits the front steps, the workings of a bicycle chain. Squawk! A squawking blackbird sounds reveille. I'm an empty flat car, third car from the rear. Three hundred and sixty-five of 'em. Stop counting, stop waiting. It's Easter, Easter fucking Sunday! Beyond the torn curtain lace there are only shadow limbs groping for the sky. Other blackbirds squawking now like a party of thieves. Fresh road kill, I heard the brakes an hour ago, screech and thu-thump! Fuckin' Rodney never knew what hit him! "If!" Another fuckin' whistle, another train in the opposite direction.

Me and Jimmy, brothers Don and Jeff, Johnny, Mule, Gonzales, Worm, and Billy Gibbons, us Dick Street Bombers, we played on them tracks. We played war, get the flag, kick the can, hot beans. We built forts under the bridge, dammed up the creek, hit homers over the fence, over the rails. We smoked cigarettes, sipped wine, talked sex. We showed each other our dicks, Johnny had the biggest. "You idiot, babies didn't never come from fuckin' storks!"

There are other birds talking now, red, blue, and gray. A coo, cooing mourning dove takes flight. The rhythmic hammer of that train passing, the heat hiss, hissing up. My cigarette ash falls to my chest. A neighbor's car whines, starts, grinding gears and drives off. I'm safe here, without really thinking, not consciously, but the night's fuckin' over. And again, we get to do it again.

I come out from my blanket, push up from my hands to my feet and stand naked before the window. There are no faces in the glass, but mine, what's only me is scary. We stretch. I'm five foot ten and all of 135 pounds. I'm apart, a part of, superimposed upon that tree, without leaves like lines of bark my ribs can be counted. When I left for the war I was 160 and flawless, but the heat, sweat, bad water and food, c-rations, and constant diarrhea made me as thin as a communion wafer, lean like a manhole cover. My eyes sunken in like a sewer rat, more black than blue anymore, my face long and narrow and missing teeth. Who is it? It ain't me, these puffs of white steam. Is it breath? Am I breathing? Or am I just a broken limb, a cut branch, kindling for the fire? Is this cover about to blow, and who will receive me?

I put my pajama bottoms on and realize I've put them on backwards. I've stopped pissing out my asshole or I'd be politically correct, could be fuckin' president. I need to make myself laugh, me and God share a laugh. There are no bunkers here, but for an old sparrow's nest under the eaves of shingle next door. I'll go ahead now and turn myself around.

Squirrels padding, pit, pat, pit, pat on the roof above, voices down below. Too much fuckin' TV. The front door creaks, and the screen door grates. My father retrieves the paper, his mumblings about it having blown apart. Yes, I have seen the pieces, bits of brain matter, all pink, and blue, and gray flesh. Just one, one patch. "Jesus," he snaps at my little brother watching cartoons, "Turn it down!" His life's so fuckin' simple—work, drink, eat, drink, sleep. "Let the dog out." Oh, and how he loves his crossword puzzle as he makes his way across the dining room, shuffling pages, into the kitchen, into his coffee cup.

The bathroom is pink and gray tiles, and too fuckin' bright. Kill the light! This piss is freedom, emancipation from one's inner demons, a moment's bliss like a yawn or a sneeze. If only for these bodily functions, is there any reprieve. A good dump is king, but for a shot of dope. "If!" What Casey already knows. I splash some water on my face but still come back orange. It's that clay, red dirt, those convoys in an open jeep, too much fucking sun.

My mother's voice rises up from the kitchen, a wafted aroma of coffee, eggs, and bacon, sizzle, pop, pop. No small arms fire here, just big appetites. Mom's cooking will soon enough fatten me up. Only last night we feasted on steak, shrimp scampi, Brussels sprouts, my favorite, and wild rice. I had two pieces of strawberry shortcake. "How was it?" she asked, and without thinking I blurted out, "Fucking great! Best fucking meal I ever fuckin' ate!"

My youngest brother and sister, Billy's seven, Marianne's nine, sat there dumbfounded, mouths agape. Everything stopped as if a rocket had hit, like someone farted in church, but you'd better not laugh. Shay, eighteen, and John, he's fifteen, took to snickering, even Dad was holding back a hoot.

"Well," said Mom, attempting to rise above the muzzled snorts, "I'm glad you enjoyed it, but I don't like that word." She tittered, giggled, and we all broke loose in wholehearted laughter.

I made my way down the stairway, downstairs, Bugs Bunny asking, "What's up, Doc?" Doc took one tiny piece of shrapnel in the temple, sitting on his cot reading a letter from home, just a head above the sandbag line.

"If!" Nothin' was up, but fucked up, and Doc's world stopped six days short of leaving. Don't mean nothin'! Still I couldn't stop the thoughts, the sleepless nights, the fuckin' nightmares. This wasn't the place I thought home would be, the war hadn't been silenced. Still, I was bored, I missed the Goddamn excitement, the killing game. This world had no meaning, no life and death consequences. Yeah, it was me who'd changed, everything else was the same only a year older. A year of hell, how could I ever again lie on a beach and tan myself.

I opened the door and stepped from the stairwell into the living room. Marianne was hiding between the upstairs and foyer doorways. Elmer Fudd was about to kill that cwazy wabbit. "Boo!" she screamed, this high-pitched screech like a rocket whistles when it's in your lap. I went up like a prizefighter does from an uppercut to the jaw, then down, down for the floorboards, stopped! Stopped myself, than snapped, snapped right the fuck out of myself! She was laughin', God was laughing. I jacked her up off her feet by the threads of her pajama top like a dog would shake a rag doll in its mouth, pinning her shoulders back up against the wall. Her eyes met my stony-cold, blackened rage! It wasn't her but the enemy I saw.

"Never, never fuckin' do that to me, never! Do you hear me?"

My mother ran in from the kitchen, spatula in hand, waving it like a scepter, a magic wand over a pimply frog, "Put her down! Put her down this minute." There were all kinds of whistles screaming in my head.

"Put her down!" My father's voice reverberated, pinging off walls, and out the back of my brain. He threw his pen and crossword puzzle at me, spilling his coffee. I'm an empty flat car, third car from the rear. Bones was snapping at my pj's. "Now!" He bellowed from a safe distance and looked to my mom as if asking, what are we gonna do now?

Billy sat bug-eyed, amused, gawking at me from the couch, this was better than any cartoon, I was cwazier than that fucking wabbit. Tears were streaming down my sister's face. What? This fear, it's mine, I thought, from the depths of the dead and the missing. My God, my God, but couldn't say it. I'd brought the trauma home. I'm the fuckin' enemy here.

◆   ◆   ◆

I spent the rest of the day and the following days in my room only coming down for meals. I didn't speak but when spoken to, kept it short and vague, and never about the war. I was estranged from the family downstairs, the sounds and laughter of kids playing on the street, a bouncing ball only gave me a headache. I tried to read but couldn't concentrate, I'd be reading the same paragraph, the same sentence over, over and again. I'd write, but just this abbreviated text, bits of information, pieces like noise in my head, and none of it made any fuckin' sense. "If!" Just these crumpled-up sheets. If I could fill the page, I thought, I'd be home free, but it was like counting days, there was always another page, another bullet hole, buttonhole to fill, another train whistle screaming off in the distance.

I took momentary naps between the nightmares, sweat immersions, and endless screams, atrocities, murderous acts I'd seen and done, some I'd never committed, or had to, or had I? Jesus, and the waking feeling of guilt, disgust, fuckin' remorse. I must be a bad person. They kept sending me back there in spite of my pleas, "I've already served, Sir, I've got metal in my leg." But no one believed me. My rifle would jam, misfire, or bullets wouldn't penetrate or stop an enemy about to kill me. Sometimes my adversaries were Americans, sometimes it was fuckin' Rodney. I'd shoot awake at the moment of dying, bleach to white as if inside Betty's last footprint, a hollowed, swallowing screech, cold, wet, empty, and stuck like death must be. Again I'd be hugging the floorboards, tied up in a blanket like a black knot, a hangman's noose.

I cleaned, arranged and rearranged my room, boxed up old trophies and sports memorabilia, and put them in the attic. Vacuumed the rug, dusted, polished, and Windexed. Stripped the walls of pictures, banners, memory, and Jesus. I pushed my mattress into one corner, then the far corner of the room, away from the light. Cleared out the closet, dresser drawers, and night table. Threw out the junk that didn't work, pens, lighters, broken shoelaces. Things I didn't need, mementos, mostly high-school shit, my old yearbook, family photographs.

I separated socks from T-shirts, short from long sleeved, jeans from fatigues, leather from corduroy, everything had to have a pocket and nothing was white. No logos, labels, image, or print, only solid dark colors with the exception of flannel. I sorted it all in neat orderly stacks and rows, and what few items on hangers, discarding anything that didn't fit, was in excess, or didn't have a purpose as a means of survival. No jewelry, not even a watch, clocks everywhere, and nowhere I'd be goin'. Nothin' to grab at from around my neck, I'd lost my cross some-time ago. I needed a belt to hold up my pants, but I'd hide it with a shirt. No fuckin' underwear anymore, suits, or dress-up clothes. I'd rent a tux for the wedding, but it would be my last wedding. No loose-fit-ting shoes but boots, and somethin' to run in. I needed to get me a new pair of ankle-high black converse, lace 'em up real tight.

Another train whistle, what used to be passengers is only freight any-more. Third car from the rear, I'm vacant and flat. Now everything had its place, and I knew where the fuck it was. Order on the outside to off-set the chaos, the splatter in my head. Sparse, almost empty as if no one lived here, no one for real. Yeah, I could fit my whole life in a fuckin' duffle bag, and be gone without tracks before the first round hit.

Three hundred and sixty-five freight cars, blemishes in the paint, where the blue hit the wall like a baseball. A year of blood, counting off days, hot metal shards, pieces, and body bags. Just one, one patch of black hair! A shadowy sun, that stain on the wall where once upon a fuckin' dream, a boy without any glass on a hillside once lay. Now, he'd been boxed forever. Half dead, survivor or otherwise. I'm all of nothin' anymore.

Soon, soon enough I'll have to get me some work, but all I'm trained to do is kill, and die. Elijah was right, what Myles would say, "We don't belong here, we can't win this fuckin' war." I could, yeah, I could go back there, let them finish the job. Kill me dead this time. And my blue, my blue block of wood. Don't mean nothin'! And into the garbage bag of disused clothes intended for the Goodwill box.

"You's be a survivor," he called out as the door closed between us. Jesus, I only wanted to cry, but no tears came. It was too fuckin' late!

◆   ◆   ◆

2

"Above the Line"

What I would do, I thought, was kill the thoughts.

◆　　　◆　　　◆

I'd been on this unemployment line for an hour or so, and there were still twelve assholes in front of me. The two behind me wouldn't shut up. Somethin' about nothin' is all they said, it was stupid like grease on grease and locker-room sweat. It was all the same banter, sex, sports, automobiles, and more sex. Banal, intrusive like paint fumes in a closet.

I am below the line like Jonah in the belly of a whale. O'Brien's suicide in a brand-new red Corvette. Off the road, and over the guardrail, out from the bridge, beneath the watermark. My world, this space like a bunker, just waiting my turn.

I might of excused myself, but didn't. I didn't really give a fuck! And surreptitiously cut wind out the hole in my ass. Waft from the seat of my jeans, a silent, deadly bomb, toxic, rancid like a dead man's last puff. Now the paint did spoil. Snowy white, ivory toothed, unblemished floor tiles, waxed and buffed, now possessed a special glow, an aura of pristine surgical excellence run amok.

That's a train whistle screaming off in the distance. I'm no more empty freight, vacant and flat, but the little red, or was it a blue engine who could and did? "Jesus," winced one asshole to the other, who whined, "My Godddd!"

Now I was the riffraff, the rabble-rouser, and just had to smile. Now I was an asshole too!

"Someone shit their pants," I said, barely audible, and remained steadfast, innocent, facing forward. Now this was fucking real, real bad, real live tears like really having to use the bathroom after your old man's been in there. Worse yet the shithouse, and having to sit alongside big fat Master Sergeant Loopahole. But most badly, I thought, Casey Jones in a soufflé of metal shards, splintered wood, meat scraps, seething blood, shit stewing. A needle for a straw, a spoon for scooping. At least this was my shit! And oh the groans, and grimacing, finger pointing, who to blame.

"Shit man, somethin' dead just popped out your butt hole!"

"It's fuckin' you man, you fucking swine!"

"Smells like your fuckin' hairy breath, that pussy you ate last night!"

Suck it up! And shut up! I thought, *or lose your place in line.* I was stoned of course, stoned again, "stoned immaculate," like the song says, like the war gave us toy soldiers license to kill. Carte fuckin' blanche! A holiday in the sun.

It wasn't that I hadn't been looking for work, but I wasn't about beating a dead horse to death. I'd have five months of this before I'd have to get a job, as if I'd fallen into grace like coins in a blind man's cup. Yes, Sir, I could do this. I was well schooled in the practice of waiting, military life and time spent away from home had learned me how. This sped-up world, fast, faster yet, only to wait your fucking turn. And there's always some poke holdin' up the show, in the wrong fucking lane, stalled in traffic, dropped his fuckin' quarter, pissed himself. Yeah, I could wait on line once every two weeks for a paycheck. These dark glasses and a head full of dope made what fluorescent, bureaucratic bullshit tolerable. Fuck you! You! And you! I'm happy to wait, just to wait my fuckin' turn. I ripped off another fart, this time with volume. An uproarious bark like a rabid dog unleashed. Come on, go ahead, fuck with me!

Nobody moved. This line wasn't moving. I felt a stab like pain to my calf like pricks from a rosebush, and could smell droplets of blood as bits, fragments of metal emerged and trickled down my pant leg. In a twinkling I possessed an astute awareness as if to pull words from someone's throat before they spoke. My name is Lazarus! Don't ask, and without moving my lips, I kept the asshole's tongue from wagging. And who's the lucky motherfucker? You're not swimming in a sea of brain matter, all pink, and blue, and gray as if it fucking mattered anymore. Just one, one patch of black shiny curls, sunken in behind one, one eye. Stuck, fixated, asphyxiated like a fuckin' knot to my fucking brain. Wreathing in the dust, all red vested, an arm up, off to the side, severed the fuck off! Sideways, shielding out one, one blue-jean eye out from a black sun. He's pointing back at himself, lookin' back at me, without any fuckin' glass. And one, once upon a fucking dream, a miss was a run. "If!" Fucking if.

"Don't mean nothin'!" Myles said.

Again, over and again. Fe, fi, fo, fum! And giants walked giant steps.

Me and Myles were safe in a bunker, a walk-in closet made of sand. Partly below ground, below the line, in the murksome rusty haze of an old beat-up flashlight. We might even survive a direct hit. "If!" If anything could. Stockwell didn't, but fuck it! "If!" And if it's your fuckin' turn, it's your fuckin' turn. Anyway, I was in the company of Ellsworth T. Myles, and truth or false, it always gave me a feelin' of being somehow invincible.

We sat facing each other a few feet apart on thin elevated planks of board, ankle deep in mud, swatting mosquitoes. It was a hundred and fuckin' thirty degrees in this coffinlike sandbox. The bug repellent we passed between us wasn't working, but only added a pungent chemical taste to an already prevalent bouquet of rat piss. It made our sweat thick and gooey. Still, this was better than dodging hot screaming metal. We were happy to be here. This was the best of places this war had to offer, heaven as we saw it, heaven's little fireball of sweltering bliss. We two lucky motherfuckers got wrapped tight in a bunker like Christmas on the Fourth of July, fireworks for Jesus, gifts of frankincense and myrrh, while giants pummeled the land. Again, thanks to Myles, who brought us here on a bad feelin' just moments before the first round hit. There were no "bombs bursting in air" like the song would have you believe. No "twilight's last gleaming," but rockets and mortars busting up what Godly fuckin' spirits, structured housing, earth, and flesh! All that was left to do was wait.

How many more assholes? Six, seven, eight, at least the two behind me had finally shut up! I hate this shit, as if I had a fuckin' choice. And again, we get to do it again.

Myles was standing over a hot plate cookin' up some potato chips when I arrived. He'd been in country three months already. He graciously offered me some, and the cot next to his where Doc last sat reading a letter from home. "Jesus," I'd burned my fucking finger on the frying pan.

"Not too salty?" he asked.

"No."

"Would have left today," he sighed like the heartfelt purr of a petted cat. "Just one, one tiny piece of shrapnel." He put a finger to the temple of his brain. "A hair, a hair above the sandbag line." God, afraid to ask, but couldn't stop the thoughts. Would I be next?

Myles wouldn't hear of it, took a liking to me, kept me under wing, my head below the sandbag line. A few years my senior, Myles was war smart by way of the streets, despite a gentle streak he was life cycles more savvy than I'd ever be. Like he'd been here before, before this, any of us, before God! When Myles said, "Incomin'!" I hit the ground. "Run!" I ran for a bunker. We did it all, everything together, all of it! He all but wiped my ass. Myles was standing on the sidelines when I lost my virginity, watchin' my back, waving and cheering me on as I rounded the bases and headed for home. We shared everything, all that was left, and split down the middle black-market profits from the sale of cigarettes, blankets, c-rations, and cases of Coca-Cola. Even by way of women, we took turns going first. I personally exacted on 'im a bad case of the fuckin' clap. Myles also imparted to me a truly deep affectionate love for Wilson Pickett. In his deejay like gospel persona, he'd go off on a rave, "If! If you got a hole! If you've got a hole in your soul! I've got a sound, a sound indeed to patchhhh it!" And from his hand held tin-can-like battery-powered cassette deck he'd blast off a song. I trusted Myles like a fuckin' dad, a big brother, my loyal dog, good old Bones. Whole fuckin' heartedly, with my life, my wallet, and my dick.

There were still five or six assholes in front of me. "Save my place in line," I grumped at the two behind, "I need some fuckin' air."

"Sure man," said the one, the other kept nodding approval. I stepped out to smoke a joint.

I'd first smoked pot "in da Nam," as Rodney put it so eloquently. After two or three rocket attacks, having to lie there and listen to the shit, with nothin' to do, I got me a bad case of da fuck-its. I might be dead before I knew it, so why not be happy and dead. I was forever flyin', got me an air medal, but this resolve soon changed. Myles didn't like me smoking on patrol, and too often pot only heightened my paranoia, or made me indestructibly stupid. I once wandered off wrongfully so, in a bad direction, almost stepped atop a bouncin' Betty, and drew enemy fire. Instead of hittin' the dirt, goin' down, I flew up and out, and blasted off on fully automatic. I sobered up three kills later, and what would later be a fuckin' bronze star. One dead gook was holdin' a sullied Polaroid of himself, his wife and kid, I traded him from my First Cav Deck for the ace of fuckin' spades. His picture went in my pocket, my card in his mouth. I propelled it home with one last fuckin' bullet.

"You's one crazy white motherfucker!" Brown exclaimed, his chin around his navel.

"Shit! You've got fucking shit for fuckin' brains!" Myles whooped down on me, smacked me on the side of the fuckin' noggin, picked my helmet up off the ground, and slammed it into my gut. "You fucking asshole!

"Short! Three days and a wake up," Rodney yelped, "I's goin' back to the world!" I'd been cuttin' off a few fuckin' ears, adornments for my necklace. "I's one lucky motherfucker!" he howled. It was his final proclamation.

◆   ◆   ◆

The shit was good, real good, bad shit man, fuckin' outstanding! Some of it laced with opium. Sometimes there where tricks that lights and shadows might play on faces in the dark, distort things off in the distance along the tree line. "Shit for fuckin' brains!" Myles put me straight, there was enough shit goin' on without me seein' or hearing things that weren't really there. I curtailed my using to those reasonably safe places, not wanting to be doing the wrong thing at the wrong time. Yeah, war's its own fuckin' nightmare, no need to be addin' jet fuel to an already hypervigilant psyche.

Jimmy'd sent me a cassette of Crosby, Stills and Nash. Stoned out, shit faced one night, sprawled out on my cot I listened to it over, over and again, back and forth, but couldn't fuckin' decipher where "Suite

Judy Blue Eyes" stopped and "Marrakech Express" started up. I played it again, over and again until I got so fuckin' disoriented I had to puke.

Abrams was wasted and started shootin' up the bush at his own troops who lay in ambush. They had no choice but to cut him down. Henderson got drunk, shot Buttkins by mistake while playin' cowboys and Indians, turned his rifle in on himself, and blew his own Goddamn head off! Smyth nodded out on guard duty, the six guys he was out on patrol with had their throats slit while sleeping. The fuckin' enemy, A.K.A. Charlie, let him live. He had to live with it, but not for long. Two months back in the world, back in fuckin' Idaho. One bright crisp fall morning, his six-year-old boy found him hanging in the barn.

Now that I was away from the war I had no fear of fucking up. Drugs and alcohol helped disarm the thoughts, quiet and calm me, helped me sleep at night. Now that don't mean nothin'! Meant fuckin' somethin'! Had surfaced like a beached fuckin' whale. In segments, memory like bits, and scraps of metal from my leg. I needed to get fucking numb. Home was a place called numb! And the world on a spit like a stoned cold dead fish.

This space here, "Jesus," it's so fuckin' overcrowded now, so many assholes out of work, a warehouse like shithouse full. Complete with Casey Jones, and big fat Master Sergeant Loopahole look-alikes. Normally I'd be overwhelmed, too big a target, too much noise, too many fuckin' elbows. I felt most alone, so lonely in a crowd. Just these damaged goods, definitively broken. But I'd had my fix! I felt nothin' as I got back in line. Four more fuckin' assholes, and it's my turn. No, nothin' works that hasn't been broken. Smyth, he's one with the sun and the rafters. Yeah, I'm leaving you now like all that's left me here.

"Money for dope, money for rope" like the song implies, "I'm sick to death of hearing things, seeing things. Had enough of watching scenes."

◆   ◆   ◆

I took the last few hits on a joint and swallowed the roach. Myles never smoked but kindly gave me a swig of his Olympia beer to wash it down. It was hot, skunked, but worked! Myles didn't drink either, but sipped, and the only time I ever saw him drunk was the night before he left, when he got all soft and mushy on me. His fix if any was for sex!

Myles had three kids back in the world, back in Baltimore by two "stunningly beautiful gorgeous babes," as he called 'em, and was in love with a third. He'd shown me their pictures, his kids, read me their letters some. "Marriage," he'd say, "don't say it, it's a baaaad word." He'd never give up any of his girlfriends. Myles needed sex at least twice a day or he wasn't himself, and more than once almost got us fuckin' killed sneaking in and around the village late at night, which was off limits and dangerous. It wasn't always for a piece of ass that I tagged along. Yeah, I was bored, I'd nothin' else to do, but I'd make him persuade me so, sweet talk me into it. Truth is I'd never let him go alone. Besides, time spent with Myles was fun, full of glorious spontaneity, accidental like happenstance, episodic fortified adventure.

We rarely paid for sex, but when we did women always came back to Myles free of charge. Women stood in line for Myles. One fifty-dollar prostitute we collectively boned eight times in one night wanted him to tie the fuckin' knot. Women loved Myles as much as he loved them. He was one of the few Americans who treated the Vietnamese cordially, not like all residents were Charlie and every woman a fuckin' whore. "They're just hungry," he'd say. "We're all gooks," he'd laugh at himself. "Niggers in a rich man's war." Myles also spoke their language some, even if it was all about obtaining a profit, or getting laid.

Boom! Railroad cars uncoupling, but it's not what I think. "Jesus!" I jump. A near hit floods the bunker with a momentary flash of brightness. The two assholes behind me hold back from laughing. It's the embedded blood spatter on my fatigue shirt they've noticed, and know better than to say or do anything. I blow out, hard, stale, heavy-laden hot air, breathe in slow and soft, and fucking cough. We try again. There are no rockets here. Stop! Am I really here? Stop! There? Stop! Stop the fuckin' thoughts!

"Motherfuckers," Myles just laughs. The splashing of mud, and that dead end sound of metal thumping sand. Myles takes up the flashlight, clicks it off, then on, off and on again toward the exit, entranceway, our only way out. "Take that you bastards!" He twirls, dips, whirls, and flips it through the air like a fuckin' baton, a liquid ballerina on the head of a fuckin' pin. Switchin' it off and on again. Off! On!

"If!"

Lights are crashin' man! Streaked and dashed like a trapeze act like fuckin' acrobats, and chariots of fire across bags of sand, and fleshy goose flesh. It's mine, all mine, the pink, and blue, and gray of it.

And fucking "If!"

I'm a rainbow juicer, crystallined, somewhere over the fuckin' rainbow. "Where bluebirds fly." Jesus, take me up! Up like Elijah fuckin' prophet! Up! I'm goin' up! Like Mickey fuckin' baseball Mantle! Up! Above the fuckin' noise! The thin fucking blue line! Like one! One fuckin' solitary teardrop! One block of blue ash!

I'm a better man! Better than Puff, Puff the Magic fuckin' Dragon! Mini-guns! Tracer bullets! "Rockets red glare! Oh, say can you see," and he who died for our fuckin' sins! Moses! David! Fuckin' Goliath! Bounce, fuckin' bouncin' Betty, and Betsy, Betsy fuckin' Ross! Buttons sown, and blown to fucking threads! I'm laughin' man! I'm fuckin' flyin'! And Myles starts in rantin', chantin' like real loud, real fuckin' loud man as if to rise above the metal storm.

"If! If you got a hole. If you've got a hole in your soul. I've got a sound, a sound indeed to patchhhh it!" And the giants are stompin', fi, fo, fum! Keep stompin' in fuckin' time. And the music starts blastin' all distorted like, like this fuckin' smile hurts my face.

"I'm gonna wait till the midnight hour! When my love comes tumblin' down!" Me and Myles join in singin' too like Tweedle Dee and Tweedle ... Fum!

"I'm gonna wait till the midnight hour! When there's nobody else around! Just you and I!" Fe, fi, fum!

"Fuck you!" Myles flashes my eyes into spotted puffs like marshmallow suns, explosions across a pitch-black sky into reality's boots. Without any fucking glass. And again it's fuckin' Rodney!

"Fuck me! Fuck me! Fuck me!" Myles snatches the flashlight in midflight, arcs it once, twice, full circle, and stops to rest beneath his chin. Clicks it off and on again, shooting light up over his face all fuckin' Halloween orange and black. He's fuckin' radiatin' man! Like a jack-o'-lantern, a fucking clown, a fuckin' headless horseman with a fuckin' pumpkin head like the minstrel bard Mr. Bones! Good old Bones. Like Emmet Kelly but with a big fat fuckin' smile, hungry white wolflike teeth, ruby fat lips, bulging tombstone ivory pools, encircling bug eyed, fuckin' blown out, big surprise! Big brown eyes! I'm laughin', laughin' so fuckin' hard now I'm cryin'.

The music unwinds, garbles, and stops. And Mr. Emmet fuckin' Kelly Bones does pontificate, "Humpty Dumpty sat on the wall, Humpty Dumpty had a great fall." Then what I think he says, "Be he alive or be he dead, I'll grind his bones to make me bread!"

Woof, wooooof! Lightning sparks like burning dogs through metal hoops. Mud splashing me up, that dead end thump, humpin' my fuckin' leg again.

"Jesus fuckers!" screams someone off in the distance, not so distant, but just outside our fuckin' sandcastle like a train whistle he's been hit. The coupling and uncoupling of cars. All I'd buttoned has fallen off. And again Myles starts in dippin', and twirlin', and fuckin' whirlin' again. On! Off! On! Jesus, I'm fuckin' spinnin' man! Like rockets go poof in the night, and Betty's last bounce. And Mr. Ellsworth T. fuckin' Myles snaps off with an uppercut to the fuckin' jaw, and Mr. Emmet Kelly fuckin' Bones clicks on.

"And all the King's horses, and all the King's men." The words move slower, dawdling now as only a memory can. "Humpty, Dumpty, together, again!" I'm fuckin' hysterical cryin', or is it laughter? The mud is percolating, even the sandbags are grinning out. "A ghost of a man, a boy, a soldier" is what I believe he says, "who are you? But the very thing you hate!"

"Stop!" I plead out, implore him with tears.

"And all the good soldiers," he asserts with a sneer, "goody, good soldiers," prodding me with the light, "died, died just tryin' to be good."

"Jesus, please!" I beg forgiveness. Accident, or otherwise, "It ain't my fault!" I bury my face in my lap. Get it together man. No more laughin', stop your crying. I take a deep breath, blow out hard, burdened, stale hot air, another, over and again. Whoa man. It's only me, me and Myles here. There is no Banquo, no more fuckin' Rodney! I wipe away the fucking tears. Yeah, yeah man. It's all okay now. No more rockets. None! No more Jesus fuckers. None whatsoever! No more fuckin' Mother Goose.

I sit the fuck up, and Myles is no more happy face, not like a fucking clown anymore. No more Mr. Emmet Kelly fuckin' Bones, but looks like Bette Davis in "Hush, Hush Sweet Charlotte." He swoops the flashlight over, above, all over me. "Jesus." He's got his fuckin' .45 pointed at my fucking head.

"Don't move!" I'm blinded like Saul from his fuckin' horse. I want to scream out, but throw the fuck up.

"Oh, my God! My fucking …" Bam!

The whole fucking place resounds in a flash like the ghostly truth before my eyes, a trigger finger to the wound in the palm of his hand. Jesus, it was me who wandered off. A rat! One giant big fuckin' decapitated rat the size of a fuckin' cat falls into my lap. A lap full of brains, blood splatter, and fucking puke. "Got it!" he laughs. "Saved your ass again."

"Hey, hey, man! It's your turn," says the asshole behind me. I snap back in line, back into myself, whatever the fuck is real anymore. The lady behind the counter looks like Bette Davis, but worse than Miss Charlotte, more like "Whatever Happened to Baby Jane." She wants to know if I've been looking for a job?

"Yes, Ma'am, there were three applications, interviews I'd had, they wanted to know where I'd been the last few years. I believe it worked against me." She asks if there's anything that I'm trained to do? "To kill and die with the best of 'em," I smirk. "Know of any job openings?" She doesn't laugh. I don't fucking care. She stamps my card unwillingly, and I'm fuckin' out of here. Above the line. "See ya."

◆   ◆   ◆

3

"Dreams Of Chasing God With a Neddle and a Bone"

Once upon a dream I was nineteen but I don't remember when. It was good I think, but ever since it's all been bad. It's overwhelming. What's too sad to comprehend, everything, all of nothin', and all of nothing else. The wrong war, the longest war, the lost war! The wrong, lost, but most beautiful girl. Who she was, might have been like one, one branch of blue sky. Is there anyone? Is there no one? Again what's all gone wrong, and again like always as if it were my fault.

"Gee God, why even a taste?"

"It's a joke you fool! Me, and the devil played," is what God told Job. "And you're the blunt of it, the raw end of the fuckin' deal! You know absolutely nothin' about the wonders of creation, the blue of branch, pink like sky, baby's pursed lips, or milky soft, silk like breast. Don't ask, how many bullet holes it takes to fill a buttonhole, whole again? Just shut the fuck up, and make the bed!"

The bed's more blood than white, and it's me who's in it! The sheets propped up on prongs like twigs, so as not to stick like feathers to a body tarred of scrapes. My flesh a grayish saffron, my eyes shot red, and yellow like broken yolks as if I'd engulfed a rotten peach, swallowed it whole. My ankles swollen like full-blown blue balloons. The ceiling drips hot wax, a truth serum like hallucination, like the whiz of burning plastic screaming into a bucket full of icy ocean. "Welcome to Club

33

Dead!" is what I think the doctor says, but I don't believe it. "This place is for anyone who's been there, who should have fuckin' died when others did!" Once, twice, "If!" Over, over and again, he repeats himself, "If! If! If! You's one lucky motherfucker. Motherfucker!"

What lines running in and out of portals like highways jammed deep inside me, pumpin' all kinds of fluids, extracting others like express trains like I'm Grand Central fuckin' Terminal! A tube up my dick, the cut of a razor's sting leaking out a black liquid Gumby bear paste into a clear cellophanelike pint-sized body bag. A wall of monitors tapping off an ever-present, constant fuckin' beep, beeping sound like a death march, like Jimmy's dad at Batton, a drum and bugle corps, foreboding like a fuckin' time bomb in my head. They'd lanced the abscess like golf ball down along my main line, among the rusty potholes and fields of ashen. Emerald pus, orange wine oozing out like a golden calf, a dying sunset, Isaac on the block. Jesus, it's the wrong fuckin' sacrifice!

Other voices, shadowed limbs, groping ghosts, faces I'd known, like mine. A melee of battle cries, you know the fuckin' names. We were all wrong! Jesus, and what the fuck for? Whistles and brains, rockets and trains, a stadium crowd cheering out a lioness roar, her voice like the last thing she said. "Get off my fucking phone!"

Over, it's over and again! Bounce, bouncin' Betty like beep, fuckin' beep! Like some stupid fuckin' sing-a-long like trying to follow the bouncing ball. "If." If only to flat line!

This is what I'd come to, all of it. And all of nothing else. Where are my angels now? Now that these bullet holes seem bottomless, eternal like hot-wired strings on some misplaced lead shod Pinocchio. One, one last mind fuck! The ambulance ride it was a chopper flight, a medivac, it was me who was screaming, Rodney's black bag fixed to my lap. Two, three cops enter, one stays at the door. "If!" As if I might be fuckin' goin' somewhere. "Assholes!" They shoot Polaroids, flash!

Without no fuckin' bang, no fiery shrapnel, photograph my arms, these tracks as evidence to be used against me. Now I see spots, Jesus in blue beneath the exit sign, a badgelike halo round a sacred bullet proof heart, and can smell my own death like Lazarus decomposing.

A corroded railroad-spike-like hurt thrust deep into my side, how she first said my name, "Curmudgeon," dropped a glob of mayonnaise from her knife to the floor. Oh my prissy, immaculate floors, and how it only made us laugh, because, just because. Was it love? Still, I love her, and what's too fucking sad! Another stab like pain, spiked, this time it's my heart like I'm being nailed to this fuckin' bed!

"Jesus!" And I ain't feelin' sorry for anyone. It's all of nothing I want to feel!

A nurse puts her palm to my chest, to absorb the quickened beat, beating of my heart. Takes my one free hand, without no strings attached, between hers, behind soft hazel eyes, in an angel's grip. It could have been her, "If!" If it weren't for a wedding band. It's what she already knows like the first time I saw Bette, tending popcorn, behind the candy counter, between the screen and her, beneath the doorway I'd been caught like a freeze frame like a corner stone arches inherently into a smile. And the movie it got fucking real!

"I ain't afraid of you," she said, and wanted to wrestle. She was young, too young, I was too fuckin' old, but couldn't help myself.

What's passed me up for a needle, and a bone!

"If!" And he who lacks any kind of commitment, any intimacy, having lost too much already, repeats himself, again, over, and again, and reaches for the unattainable. No, nothing gets too close! I'd been fucked! Diseased! Me, you, we've all been quarantined!

"Be still," says the nurse in a voice like chapel bells, and the wind chimes off in the distance, calls my name like a subterranean train whistle. All I'd left to do was shut my baby blues real tight. Look on down from the bridge.

◆   ◆   ◆

I was all of eight, and running up the hill from the creek to the tracks, firing backwards at Jimmy, "Bang, bang! You're dead!" Oblivious I turned as the train shot past, sucked in my face, "If!" If only for a moment, and spit me out backwards, upside down, back down the hill, wrong side up.

"When my love comes tumblin' down!" A negative slam dunk like Jack without Jill, and a bucket full of nothin'!

My dad was on that train, day in, day out. A drunk who went to work each day, came home to cocktails already half in the bag, and passed out in his easy chair most nights, the TV still booming. He never said much, was there I guess but mostly absent, mostly just repeated what my mom had to say. Sometimes he'd disagree, they'd argue, he'd get twisted up like knots, knotted up in some nostalgic bender, romanticizing what the fuck, and didn't know the truth of it. "Back in my day," he'd whine and grumble, wouldn't make no sense, say whatever, stupid shit.

It was our birthday dinner, I was born on his twenty-fifth. He was on a jag about an umbrella Marianne had given him, getting all sentimentally mawkish, no one had ever given him an umbrella before. My mom said something about Aunt Anna giving him one when they first got married. "No, no, no," he insisted, "she gave me galoshes!" They bickered back and forth. My sisters sided with my mom, us boys kept quiet.

Wild Bill was on a toot again, making nonsense, might as well have been blathering at his food. The women folk blasted away, shot him full of sarcastic barbs, endeavored to laugh him off. Five-year-old Billy was standing behind my dad, out from his view, in an attempt to open the umbrella it only opened halfway, turned inside out on itself, it's metallic veins sticking up above the cloth like broken wings on a dead bird. Wild Bill raised his two fists like six shooters into the air. "This is my very first umbrella!" We all broke loose in frenzied laughter, howls and snorts, he didn't have a fucking clue, must have thought we were chortling at him. He was lost, too drunk, verging on a wet brain, defenseless, started muttering to himself, and fell face down in a plate of mashed potatoes, meatloaf, and lima beans.

My mom was forced to wear the pants, pull the family up by her bootstraps. She was an overbearing, domineering nag who asked too many questions, always knew fucking best, but was still my only confidant. She'd size up my girlfriends like a shopping list, dishonest, immature, insecure, she's a phony, too much makeup, that one needs a hairbrush, and none of 'em were good enough. And me, I could never be as good as Jimmy, he'd ask his mom what she needed from the store without her asking.

My mother once confided in me, "I'd have left your father years ago if it weren't for the kids." Jesus, what could I do about it? I'd run away before, but I needed to run away for good.

My father never fought in WWII like all the other Dick Street Bomber dads. A childhood disease left him with a punctured eardrum, he was classified 4F. He even wore a goofy woman's bathing cap with daisies on it when we went swimming, made him look like a wiffle ball, but it kept the water out of his ear. He was loud, obnoxious, couldn't hear himself, you'd have to scream at him! "What?" he'd say, lean in on ya, and you'd be putrefied by too much Old Spice. Still he was virtually harmless, and never once, ever raised a hand to me.

He'd be yelling from the stands, drunk, repeating himself, discombobulated like embarrassin' stuff. I'd be tryin' to play the game. I'd ignore him, he'd keep calling my name. He was so loud he'd be the only person you'd hear among a cheering crowd. Go home dad! I'd wished he'd stayed home, I felt nothin', nothin' but ashamed. He cared, yeah, he cared alright, but just didn't know how to, not without slurring his words.

I knew the military would provide meals, housing, and a paycheck. Get me the fuck outta the house. I tried enlisting in the Marines but they said I'd have to wait three months, so I crossed the street and joined the Army. Eighteen, and two days out of high school I left home. Nine months later I was leaving for Vietnam, I'd volunteered.

My mom didn't want me to go, knew the war was one giant blunder. My dad was too fogged, hungover, in his cups to have any opinion. When I said goodbye we shook on it. I never even kissed my mom. As I looked back from the street and waved she was standing in the doorway crying. I wanted no part of her tears. None whatsoever. I had to be someone different, other than my dad, to be the man he'd never be. John Wayne, like Audie Murphy. I wanted to be a fuckin' hero!

◆   ◆   ◆

I'd been walking backwards now some fifteen years, these same dead roads, back and forth, thumb extended, spread across nooks and crannies, paving ghosts like butter melts on an English muffin. I'd been calling nowhere my home. This monsoonlike rain, red brick tears like spigots of blood that won't stop, that white picket fence like a crown of thorns, and Jesus, whose fuckin' sins are these? It's all a fucking lie! My worst, most deadly, costly mistake was volunteering for anything. I don't believe you! I don't want to play anymore! It ain't my fuckin' fault!

A pin prick razor pinch like piss burning, a snippet of liver. Rivers flood, mud swells, wanes, gulps, and swallows me up. Again I must be leaving. This place, school, city, town, job, and hospital bed. This fucking world is wrong side up. Street signs, mile markers like body bags consumed, counted off, billboards, monitors, heartbeats, and fleshy parts spiraling downwards in a whirlwind flush. "Chicken Little the sky is falling."

Movement is the constant flow of images, screens like windshields evaporating attention and leaving no place of reminiscence. Now that just past, in passing, was, isn't anymore, has been replaced and holds no contemplative realm. And here it's all about what freedom might be like "If." But every stop again is caught, and from behind turns again, a rush of memory like wave upon waves, dragging me undertow. I am bedridden, cursed, ill fated, to be the very thing I hate. Still, lost, stuck! A ghost of a man, a boy, a soldier. Jesus, is this all there is? I'm goin' fuckin' nowhere.

Empty minds in packed cars keep watch, heaters blastin', kept aglow as Yossarian melts into the plaster screen of a drive-by movie. Other cars, minds and hearts hiss past, tinted glass, swish, passing me by. Sewage drains like blood gutters, drain pipe dreams, it's all goin' down! We who once were soldiers are homeless anymore. The best of the hitchhikers. I am the Nomad King.

Short abbreviated steps, reasoning prowess like words on a page, the condition of music, thumb to the fuckin' sky. Dependent upon a genie, the genius of generosity like one, one good Samaritan. Please kind Sir, I'm only tryin' to get back to somethin', or is it to get away from? These splotches of mud, metal bits, my fleshy goose self. And this piece, it ain't even a piece, won't fit that fuckin' puzzle, make me whole again. Who I once was, I'm not, will never be I guess. It's over, over and again, but what's forever, eternally left unbuttoned? Jesus, how many more bullet holes before I disappear? To be, or not to be one lucky motherfucker. Swishhhhhh.

I once traveled from Phoenix to New York in five hours less than three days. New York to San Francisco in eight days, that with spending twenty-four hours in an Indiana jail. I'd been riding with two escaped convicts. Their car, credit cards, even their greasy overalls were stolen. I knew they were loose, somethin' was up, but I was makin' the trip with thirty dollars in my pocket, and the threads on my back. I'd be the last one asking any questions. Fortunately for me because they told the cops I knew nothing. It was the truth. Did get my meals gratis, two hotel stays, and two states further down the highway. That night one of the convicts picked the cell lock with a shoelace. I stayed put knowing I'd be released soon enough. They never did make it past the desk sergeant.

I'd told the police chief my name was Moses D. Prophet, I had the hair, the beard, looked like Charlton Heston, but he didn't believe it. He'd suspected I'd run off, escaped from a mental hospital. I gave him another name, Charlie Darwin, he checked out missing persons, and let me go the next morning.

From San Francisco to Reno, met a babe at the roulette table, got me three free days, a place to rest, food and sex! Got a union job in Boise with fake ID plugging holes in a concrete wall. From Boise to Old Bisbee, collected stones, stole a miner's wife and shot across the border like Geronimo. Back to Tombstone, left her there. Smuggled drugs into Boulder, Cheyenne, met a waitress, ate some mushrooms, just had to leave. Philly, New York, Boston, Chicago, keep moving, L.A., Vegas, Salt Lake, before whatever it is catches up with me. Again, back and forth like some broken slinky without no fuckin' steps like a song that skips.

What I like best about hitchhiking is meeting people I'd never have to see again. Late at night it gets real intimate, personal like you can say whatever, tell dark secrets, feel cleansed, absolved, close, comfort each other on a first-name-basis only. And where the road forks we split like two, and go our separate ways. I'd delight in such stories of children, wives, careers, homes, appliances I'd never have. Sometimes they'd let me drive. These strangers I'd talk to about almost anything, "If." If I felt inclined, I'd be tolerated, sometimes I'd mention the war.

It's a hobo's life without the trains, braving the elements, enduring weariness, legalities, poverty, and famine, but coffee works wonders, kills the appetite. I learned to drink it, stay awake, keep moving. My Cheyenne waitress kept me in from the snow and the freeze, kept me in caffeine all night until her shift ended. "Don't fall asleep in my booth in case the boss shows up, don't want no trouble." Man, I was so fuckin' tired, at one point I wandered into the bathroom, sat on the toilet, crossed my legs, put my head in my hand, my elbow resting on the toilet paper roll, and fell asleep. I dozed off for only about ten minutes, when I awoke my legs were all rubbery like, like pins and needles. I had to pee real bad. I wobbled out, twisted up, more tired than awake, unzipped my pants looking for the urinal, there was none. Fuck! I was in the ladies' room.

Why the fuck is it that Moses never got there? Forty fuckin' years, and he only got to see it from a mountain top. Why the fuck is God so Goddamn angry? What the fuck did Job ever do other than being righteous? "It's a joke you fool!"

And me, I ain't nothin', no nothin' but sinful. And here there are no fuckin' rules. But only for the Ten Commandments of Thumb.

1. Always travel alone! I'd learned this the hard way. A babe may get you rides, but she's easy prey. In the long run she'll only slow you down.

2. Thou shalt not smoke, it's gangsterish, or put a hand in pocket no matter how cold. Potential rides are a leery lot, might suspect a concealed weapon.

3. Thou shalt stand open, legs apart, arm extended, thumb held high, but not too high. Greet your would-be driver with soft eyes, a warm but quaint smile.

4. Thou shalt always be moving. Thou shalt not be idle. If stuck at an entrance ramp tread softly backwards with oncoming traffic, between cars take up the slack, as a vehicle approaches step back again in the direction you wish to be going. Movement begets movement, begets a ride.

5. Thou shalt never carry more than one bag. Preferably a duffle bag. Rides are not moving company's, don't wish to be burdened with all that much stuff. The lighter your load the quicker you'll travel.

6. Thou shalt come to know the best way to get a ride is to already have one. In the presence of your driver you are believed a good passenger. If you stop for food or gas talk it up with strangers, ask where they're going. "For by this some have entertained angels without knowing it."(Heb.13:2) I'd be sitting at a coffee counter, in the passenger seat, or cleaning a windshield, my ride he'd be getting off at the next exit, and I'd find me another going two hundred miles further down the road.

7. Thou shalt not ride with a drunk unless he gets in the backseat and lets you drive. He'll be asleep when you get to where he's going. Park at a rest stop, leave the keys in the ashtray, empty his wallet of all but ten bucks, enough to get home. Leave him his credit cards, and he'll think of you as kind.

8. Thou shalt stay off deserted, darkened roads late at night. Work the coffee shops, and well-lit entrance ramps. Get friendly with waitresses, they'll get you rides. In bad weather, by light of day thou shalt venture off down the highway. If you're close to a truck stop, or any type of refuge it works against you, but out in the middle of fuckin' nowhere someone will have pity on your ass, and give you shelter from the storm.

9. Thou this be obvious, I've seen a lot of fuckin' idiots out there. Thou shalt always leave room available for a potential ride to pull over, and pick you up.

10. Always carry a weapon.

◆   ◆   ◆

"Blood be thicker then water," Pop-Pop would say. I had no family left. No tree of life, or any good had come of it. My father the drunkard! No hallowed ground, but a wasteland of bomb craters, wine bottles, shell casings, body counts, and couch slumps. Fuzzy TV lines, unemployment lines, static like talking ghosts, puppetry strings, just enough wire, just enough rope. And out from the mine fields, and over the guardrail, beneath the water mark, it ain't grandma's house we're goin' to. Not this time.

I'd grown up in a small suburban town, believed in God, was a Dick Street Bomber, and marched with my Little League team in the Memorial Day parade. We all laughed when Mr. G. our coach, waving and smiling off to the sidelines, flopped his sandaled foot into a steaming pile of horse shit. Still, despite my dad's drinking, I'd respected adults, intuitively believed grownups knew best. Vietnam was my first time away from home. What hopes, naiveté, imaginary worlds of cars, trucks, little green soldiers I'd played in the roots of the old oak tree were all roped, gutted by the misery of war. All those forts I'd built, toppled so, I'd gone and run off from a burning house and into the fires of hell. Now it all seems like a bad dream I can't wake the fuck up from.

The likes of big fat Master Sergeant Loopahole, and his cohort of amoral lifers, lowlife, career fucks, made my dad look saintly. My father never missed work, was never cruel, promiscuous, or physically mistreated anyone. He'd say stupid shit, had a boozed heart, but at least it was in the right place. The drunken escapades of Loopahole and his associates included both thievery and bribes, murder and rape. One night driving drunk he and Miranda flipped a jeep, rolled it over, over a Vietnamese woman. She'd been killed, but they shot her anyway, shot her and the vehicle up with bullet holes, said she was Charlie's wife, they'd been ambushed. They both got fuckin' purple hearts. They even had a sick fuckin' distorted sense of bravado, and were braggarts about it.

And me, who knew the difference, I became the very thing I hated. I'm nothin', no, nothin' but that starving woman's bag of food slop I'd taken away, and pushed down in the mud. She'd slobbered all over me, "My baby son, for baby son!" I knew she was hungry, but she might be feeding the enemy.

That fuckin' gook barber who'd cut my hair one afternoon, I'd shot one night coming through the wire. And once upon a fuckin' haircut he'd told me, "Don't care if Communist, or fuckin' Capitalist, who wins shit war, only want stop this fighting." I'd fuckin' stopped it for 'im.

That kid running toward me, all smiles, happy fuckin' face, "GI number one! Number fuckin' one GI!" He'd raised a fist, his arm swung back, Jesus, I swore it was a fuckin' grenade, but it was a Goddamn apple. That's how Donny Gains got it, and I wasn't gonna be next. Don't mean nothin'!

And again what Myles said, "Better to be alive and sorry than be fuckin' dead!"

I'd been foolin' around with this Vietnamese interpreter, jokingly pinched him, and he pulled a knife. Cut my hand as I jumped back, my fatigue shirt pocket. I drew my .45, didn't ask, reason, barter, or fuckin' hesitate. I'd learned to never pull a gun without shooting first. Bam! I'd gone and wrapped his fuckin' brains around his Goddamn face like a Christmas package. The pink, and blue, and gray of it splashin' all over me.

Over, over and again!

You just didn't know who the fuck anyone was. Even myself anymore, whose side I was on? I shot it all! Shot stray dogs, pack elephants, water buffalo, eventually I'd shoot myself up! Wrong side up. Sold them dead dogs to the Vietnamese for five bucks, and didn't care if they were feeding Charlie.

Me, now I ain't nothin', no nothin' but dead meat, metal bits in a rice pilaf of blood juice and human waste. Yeah, anybody want a piece? And you pick me out from your teeth like a sliver of red moon, a frag-like poppy seed, a black sun on a pitched fork. I ain't anyone's relation. And mud, mud is thicker than blood.

◆   ◆   ◆

Beep, beep, fuckin' beep! I'd opened my eyes to a smiling nurse. I was tangled up in my own life lines, and had shit myself again. Somehow she made it all seem okay. Somehow I believed her when she said it would be.

◆   ◆   ◆

The drugs and alcohol didn't work anymore, wouldn't stop the thoughts. I needed more, and things only got worse. No, nothing past the rush, beyond the blackouts, not even a moment's sway. I needed to pass out to fall asleep, and still the nightmares. No, nothing could stop the war, and I couldn't stop the drugs. I was worse than my fucking dad.

Tracks like bullet holes up and down my arms, another rusty railroad spike shooting me up, but it ain't enough! This runny nose, aching bones like I need another shot like I need to breathe. This life I only live to use, use to live, but I ain't alive. Half dead, survivor or otherwise. I'm all of nothin' anymore, but for all of nothin' else.

Again I'd be tryin' to kick, having already been kicked too much like a kicking horse kicks a wounded dog. No place I'm goin' to, but going. Nothin', no nothing but dead-end space like black sucking gaps in the mud. This wind at my face driving me backwards, threads like sac cloth being torn away, blown apart. Holes, and more holes, holes in my pockets, and any attempts at change fall through. No nothing ever good it seems that doesn't come undone, or is it these knots, knots itself up? It's what I deserve, nothin', no nothin' but the worst of it. What last shot like the memory of God, who ain't come back! "Yes Sir, yes Sir three bags full," and sogged to the fuckin' bone.

I could die here if no one stops, curl up on the side of the road like a swirl of dog shit, go frozen white like an ice cream cone, or under a bridge in a cardboard box where once were soldiers bury themselves alive. Who would know, there was no one.

I'd left to put out the trash, and never brought in the mail like the button and unbuttoning of shirts, I was tired of pooping. I'd thrown out what empty liquor bottles, spent needles like busted-up old guns, bent, burnt coffee spoons like black sterling halos that merge beneath the flesh, and soften the blows. I'd been sucked up through cotton balls, poured out bottle spouts and left without leaving a note, or any trace of leaving as if someone still lived here, and had just stepped out for a quart of milk. And the drug pushers, the landlord, bill collectors, they'd all eventually come looking for their money. I'd lost that shovel the shit job. Sold what I could, drank it up, sold my blood, shot me up! There was no money. I'd nothin' left to do but run.

That last phone call, what she said, and didn't say, and how she couldn't fix me. And I can't fix her. It! Anything! Now nothing works, and everything's broken. Jesus, can't get me up off the floor, and there's no bounce, but for bouncin' back like Betty does and always will. I didn't choose to be here, who would die, and what "If!" If only for the last time. And again like always as if it were my fuckin' fault.

"We don't belong here," Myles would say it, say it over, over and again. "We can't win this fuckin' war!" Now there's nowhere I belong.

"If!" And if I knew then what I'd come to be, I'd have never left, as if this war had ever left me. Now I need to stop the substances like I need someone to stop, pick me up, stop this raining metal storm, these giants from stompin', stop my fuckin' brain, beep, beeping! Please kind Sir, pull me out from myself. Out from between these double yellow lines, from between the pink, and blue, and gray of it. And this war like concrete divides, separates me from life, barricades me off, meridians myself from being anything. But is there no joy, no happiness? Who she was, might have been like one, one branch of blue sky. No! But for one, one patch of black shiny curls, sunken in behind one, one eye swimming in a sea of brain matter. Severed the fuck off! Lookin' back at me, pointin' accusatory like. And this piece, you know, what ain't, and isn't anymore. And who will part the blood red sea? And who will make me whole again?

These stuccolike veins, and there's blood on the ceiling having shot the clot that jammed me up. Blood everywhere, plaster dripping, and the rot, rottenness of dead toilet tissue like human flesh. I can't stop shred, shredding toilet paper like these fleshy parts scattered all about me. A sea of dead flesh. Stop! One, one distant finger like a train off track scraped atop a kitchen table top, over, over and again, that same fuckin' spot. "If! If! If!" If what you lucky motherfucker?

Load it up, having missed the mark, that shot. Load it up again, over, over and again. And again. I don't give a fuck!

Jesus!!! I'd convulsed with the spike still in my arm, whacked my fuckin' head on an A-frame beam, ripped the Goddamn kitchen sink faucet out from its foundation just tryin', tryin' to hold the fuck on tight. What spastic flailing, earthquakelike seizure rising up like volcanic ash, a violent force diving me backwards, propels me, attempts stuffing me down the Goddamn fucking toilet. Off with the towel rack! One, one foot in the crapper. Off, off with the shower curtain, and curtain rod. "If!" And if I can get to the fucking floor it'll stop all this preverbal kicking, what demons abound, pound, pounding me back, powdering me into slag. It's my fuckin' soul it wants. And again it's the shit, and the piss, and the mud's the best place to be.

Now to just lie here in icy bathwater until the giants stop their stompin'.

Yes, I've tasted the blood so many times before, having died so many times before this. I'd been down, rang the bell, disrupted plumbing, split seams, but never stayed down for the count. Who is it? Who's laughing? Who's taken my place? "Jesus!" And where's my turn?

"Just shut the fuck up, and make the bed!"

Me and Job, we'd cursed the fuckin' day we were born, but never did dare curse God. Not once, not "If!" And it's the repetition that's killing me, faces like Rodney's, over, but it ain't over, it's me, like all the rest, across the page and blackboard sky, metal frags, bloody faucets, patches, bits, it's all backed up. And this shit won't flush. "Shit!"

Dime bags, body bags, bullet holes, and empty fuckin' gin bottles. Almost, but not enough. "If!" If only for a hotshot like Casey, Casey fuckin' Jones at the Goddamn throttle. Woof! Wooooof! One, one good rocket. But to fall off like swine from a cliff, out from the madman, and over the bridge, beneath the water mark in a brand-new red Corvette. And Smyth, he's one with the sun, and the rafters. "If!" And again to be perfect like the first and last thing, to be born again dead eternally grateful.

This ride ain't saved me, it's the same stranger in passing. He tells me everything, all of nothin', and all of nothing else knowing we will never meet again. He pretends to understand, but can't fix me. Another road-stop shit house. Again what last shot. And the cooker smells like gunsmoke, of burnt flesh, that killing rush like God's own hand, and this killing me joke. And how she deceived me into believing I'd be whole again like one, one branch of blue sky. "If!" And the fucking memory of, or is it just so that I don't give a shit. Why the fuck? "If!" Why does it always have to be somebody else who fuckin' dies? No! No nothin' works that hasn't been broken. And who is it that left me here? Yet unfinished. Jesus, this must be fuckin' hell.

◆   ◆   ◆

The nurse was feeding me soup. She'd asked if I had a name, but it was hard enough to swallow. I knew who I was, but didn't wanna be me anymore. "Open," she says. I'll be you, I thought, yeah, we'll be happily ever after.

◆   ◆   ◆

She'd stopped answering the phone. And Bette, Betty she's a land mine bounced up and down in my lap, cut me like him in fuckin' two! And Rodney never knew what the fuck was up like "what's up, Doc?" Who's no longer short, but the short of it like these pieces don't fit, won't put Humpty Dumpty together again. Make me whole again. It's that war, this war, that girl, just, just because. Still, I love her, and like before, before this, and the difference, the distance like always goes unnoticed, or is it pinning my ears, my ass to the wall? It's just too fuckin' sad.

Jesus, it's only me here, ain't nothin' else out there, no nothin' but empty vacant space, all knotting me up like string into wire, all balled wax, dripped flat, run out. It's over, really over, but here it fuckin' comes again. Who the fuck is it? Why this? You're absolutely alone, what purposelessness, without meaning, no nothin' but nothin' to be done about it. Red tears and fleshy parts, and the sky splits, spits, metal bits and shards of glass into goosey rhymes, puddles like spilt milk. It's spoiled!

And when I went there she called the cops, cops with sling shots who stole my ID like I was Goliath. I saw only war machines, machine gun fire, you know the bounce, bouncin' like I was like a fuckin' bob, bobbing head. Puff! And I disappeared like magic smoke, dragon's breath, without a trace, tracerlike bullet like I was the fuckin' holiest of holy ghosts. I ran off like gutter waters, blood gutters, down deserted fuckin' streets, Jesus, fuckin' out there! Beyond the distance, difference, unnoticed like blue lines on a blank page. Across fields and jungle paths, back alleys, barbed wire, high weed, rice fuckin' patty, distilled swamps, tall buildings, dilapidated shacks. Archways, corner stones, doorways marred in lamb's blood. We are the first born of a lost war, a seething metallike lioness grip, the marrow of a warrior, the curse of David. Thou shalt not house the Lord! And to pass, in passing, what's blood soaked, black on blue, gray flesh, baby's pursed lips, what's greater than the fuckin' day. No! No nothin' anymore are the colors of Noah's all-inclusive gratuitous rainbow.

I wrestled a black man at midnight wielding a steak knife like Satan's own angle of death. Kicked him down a flight of steps, and left my bayonet in his throat. I wanted to fuck him, pull out the blade and fuck 'im in the hole. In his fuckin' Adam's apple, in the place of original sin. Fuck me whole again!

I heard voices like sirens, scantily clad virgins, a jeering crowd screaming out a train-whistle-like lioness roar, out the back of my fucking brain, beep, beeping! A ruinous coliseum, scintillating, thumbs down motherfucker! I escaped via the fire escape his boot print on my cheek, a meaningless kiss.

It's not her, but the possibilities of her I'm missing. What I can't remember like what I can't forget! No nothin', not until what I haven't grabbed at leaves me for good like water out from under a bridge, the last thing she said, all that's been lost. My God, it's collectively flawed, splat, pining into mud, heavenly fuckin' mud pies. Is it all in what I can't have? Could it have been anyone? This merry fuckin' go round, that brass ring, this monkey! And I just had to fall off, dizzy like, I just had to fuckin' puke. And again I'd strung myself out on a naked limb, without a rope, meaningless, less than Judas, who at least hung himself with a garden hose, but for watering a crown of thorns.

◆   ◆   ◆

The nurse had left me here some hours ago. It wasn't any good now being awake. The only hose I'd left was fixed to my groin, humpin', pumpin' a fuckin' dialysis machine, pimpin', churning my blood. The guy laid out to my right had no fuckin' legs, he'd been comin' here three times a week for the last eleven years. At his suggestion I'd slept it off. It didn't hurt any, but sucked. All these TVs blastin' soap operas in Spanish, a gymnasium full. "Fuck!" This is what I'd come to, all I'd left me here.

◆   ◆   ◆

I'd held up this grocery store, sixty dollars and twenty-six cents and a bottle of mad dog 20/20. Because, just because, I didn't like the way the clerk stared me down. Impulsively, on a whim like I was Jimmy Cagney like Humphrey Bogart with a stiff finger stuck out from under my raincoat. Like God I put the fuckin' fear of God in 'im.

Stole an idling Porsche and sped off like Mario Andretti, crashed it downtown, center square under the big marquee like James Dean, trampled the petunias, the fuckin' marigolds, and over a concrete barrier into a WWI statue of a doughboy five sizes bigger than life. It's all a Goddamn fucking lie! His knees buckled, he toppled over, his big fat metal-helmeted head smashed through the windshield like a meteorite, plopped down beside me, swallowed the stick shift and gear box whole like Linda fuckin' Lovelace, Jesus, the whole twelve inches! "Nice to see you again," I said, facetiously. "Yours was a war to end all wars, yeah, right motherfucker!" And I split as if in two like mirrored tricks and sleight of hand, within, and without you. Again I escaped mostly unscathed, but for a cut above my left eye. A hissing gash like vapor, and into the slippery steam of a busted radiator block like breath from a manhole cover. Poof! Inexplicable orange smoke. Like I'm a bunny into a hat, a rat unto a sewery birth.

Down here there are no names remembered, but faces like advertisements on shopping carts full of empty bottles and cans. Mr. Hefty Bag Man, wrapped complete, tight, knotted up like a Christmas package of charcoal, and bitters, a bad, bad fuckin' boy in black body sacks, his boots held on with rubber bands. Mr. News Print Man, hunched back, backwards over the fire massaging his big fat ass with yellowing fingers. His hollow rags chockablocked with the Sunday *Times* like a scarecrow whose straws been picked, pecked too much by nonbelievers, disenchanted, squawk, squawking blackbirds. Mr. Dog Eat Dog Man and his twelve disciples all warm and supple in a huddle of live fur, crunch, scrunching up some Kibbles and Bits like fishes and loaves of bread. A man sprouting trees, branches, and dead leaves, bronzed, orange, some dangerously pointed. A woman of scarves winds a long and flowing gait, her transistor radio plays melodically up close to her ear. "And the blue flies circle your head like stars. I am King here. Tied to this heart by the King's chain." An androgynous thingamajig, a space junkie in blue baggy sweats and red ballerina slippers dances to and fro, out of time, legs, arms, fingers flailing about as if trying to undo a knot. "Jump into me now. I must not see the water." Whatever it be beneath astronaut headgear, black tinted visor, wearing black evening gloves, twists and turns spastically at knobs of air into doorways of no exit, no way back. "She lashed at her own skin, so she would be the Master." It confiscates like a ravishing gale from the woman of scarves a crumpled-up Wonder Bread bag, and leaps atop a milk crate. In a shrill, muffled snarllike rasp it speaks out against the rats.

Trains are passing back and forth. "I will feed you, so you don't eat me." It scatters what few crumbs among a gathering horde. "Momma says if I feed the rats, I'll save my toes!" It laughs a dark wailing cry like slow winding chalk across a blackboard sky, "Hee, heee, heee, heee!" Trains subside in the distance, and wing-tipped lights cease there pulsing.

The Rag Man Magician in quilted cape and century-old dread locks gestures wildly at the third rail as if it were somehow responsible, waving a magic wand of broken-off turnstile. "We are the rats. We are the fucking rats!" He pulls the magazine section out from Mr. News Print Man's gut, a branch of dead leaves from the man sprouting trees, a purple scarf off the nape of the woman of scarves, and tosses them up sanctimoniously like a burnt offering to the fire. "Rats! Cats! Cats! Rats!" He barks, and shakes his head willy-nilly. Now I know what's boiling in the pot. "Here scarecrow, catch this!" He hurls a ball of reddish, yellow flame, and Mr. News Print Man bursts bright orange like a dying sunset, chariots afire!

"Elijah, take me up!"

◆   ◆   ◆

Was it the bed next to me, his TV, some movie soundtrack, or just a bad dream? Was it the doctor, the nurse talking? Was it all in my head? The cut above my left eye had them believing I just might be John Doe 151. I couldn't open that eye. It wasn't the physical pain, but what lay emotionally beyond repair, knowing she'd never speak to me again. I'm unaware who's telling you this, I don't want to be the one. The lucky motherfucker! What Bette said, this war, its intrusiveness, a lion's share, Achilles heel! All I'd lost, and the last of it waiting to die. It's wherever the fuck I am, anything anyone might say. I don't know the day, month, or year of it! Whose face is on the dollar bill? Whose God we trust! Who freed the fuckin' slaves?

They leave. I flag the nurse, she shuts off the TV. My roommate doesn't watch TV, but listens, doesn't talk much, but laughs a lot, an androgynous laugh. He spits constantly into a brown paper bag he carries around with himself like a cuddly teddy bear. I open my one good eye. "You laughin' at me?"

"No man, I'm a chopper." Twirls his arm above his head. "Whoop, whoop, whoop." Laughs, and spits again. "Firebombs man, hells fire.

Hee, heee, heee, heee!" He sweeps his left hand, his arm swinging just above the floor as if shooing away dust, lost stuffing, or cellophane from a cigarette wrapper, that's what I think, but there ain't nothin' there.

"What is it, man? Get shot down?"

"Body parts." He's serious, continues sweeping. "Arms, legs, pieces, they're fuckin' everywhere!" He goes stiff like a bird unwittingly smacks itself into picture window glass, starts convulsing.

Me, I can't fuckin' move. "Nurse!"

◆   ◆   ◆

Above ground I'd found myself rifling through a dumpster lookin' for a syringe I'd thrown out the night before. Mistakenly, I found God! He looked like a scarecrow, but instead of straw his flesh was frayed and his bones were showing. He looked like me like Lazarus, but more dead than alive like Jesus crowned and bloody whipped. His hair slicked back in thick braided knots like where the sky meets the tracks like a hangman's cord like a transformer burning orange. Snap, crackle, sizzle, pop!

The sky was black and mirrored all about me. Rotting posts like puppets dangled from telephone wire, taunted, haunting me without moving their lips. Cracked ribs, metal bits, shards of glass, eroding chunks of parking-lot pavement, weeds stuck out, a set of disused tracks, a Safeway all boarded up like visions of Armageddon. Again my leg was leaking.

And I saw in him all the pain I'd ever felt, the hurt, the losing end. "What the fuck are you doin' here?" He didn't answer, but I knew he'd come for me. It might have been the drugs, that I hadn't eaten or slept in three days, but at that moment I realized death was no escape. "If!" If I were to die here nothing would stop, not the war, who she was, might have been. Jesus! I'd be as empty, as hollow but worse. A gutted ravenous fiery pit for all that eternity brings.

Like Moses with a stick like water from a brick, and out from under a crushed doll's head, an old rusted-out Schwinn bicycle frame I found a Chinese buffet, chicken and peanuts, broccoli and shrimp, greasy spareribs. I started eating. It was then that God was miraculously transposed, resurrected, divinely transported from a scarecrow into an antique. A beat-up tarnished lamp stand, a soiled shredded lampshade of orange and blue twine. "I don't fuckin' believe you!" But I didn't know who or what to believe anymore.

It was late, too late, but I went back to her place. I left a letter in blood, dipping into the sole of the boot stomp, the cut above my left eye. Something about love, war, how I hated her now. And where the fuck are my angels? I found an Ivory soap sample in her mailbox, and wrote in bold broad script across her picture window glass, **I am the last dead soldier left alive.** I took, or rather left a shit on her welcome mat, and wiped my ass with her phone bill.

Jimmy was dead a week already. An overdose. He'd done the laundry that afternoon, left his wife a love poem, a dozen red roses. He'd felt complete, good about himself. That night our favorite barkeep had to break down the bathroom door. He'd gone blue, blue all over. He'd given me my first shot some years earlier, stood above me sitting on the toilet seat. Spinning in space I'd buried my head in his arm pit like a burning bush, the voice of God. It was all good. I'd given him his last shot, he took it with him like God's own answer. He didn't know, I knew he'd fucked her. That final fix! It was a fuckin' accident, "If!" Even if I was happy about it.

Me, I had to tell his mom at three A.M. The cops gave me an hour, and I thought it best she hear it from me. "Jim is dead." A moment's shock, and she wailed like a stuck pig, gasped and grabbed at air, arms and hands, fingers flailing about empty spaces for the why of it. As if death had a reason, life were somehow fair. Tears, uncontrollable pink, blue, and red tears!

"My boy, my poor boy!" She'd thought he'd stopped using. His wife, she was three months pregnant. That promotion at work, senior VP. Their new split-level home, a brand-new red ... no! That's fuckin' O'Brien. "His first born," she blubbered, "will never, he'll never, God, I'll never see him ..." Her words trailed off into giant sobs, panting gulps as if sucking through a straw for the life of him. She pounded her fist, her head, her entire being against the wall, a wall of transparent places, a wind of her own making. Against and into nothing. Against what meaning, the purposelessness, the fucking guilt. Convulsing against the news, against believing. Against the why, the if, and why the fuck not!

This was a first for me being a messenger, I'd always before ever been a bag man. And this piece, it's worse than baggin' Rodney. "If!" And if my mother had to go through this. Said somethin' like a silent prayer she'd never have to, but made no fuckin' promises.

War possessed no interval of grief, no time for the dead, but only for stayin' alive. Death be dead, really dead! And death be tolled without intellect, no fuckin' church bells, draped flags, baggy pipes, ain't no explanation to be had, it's un-fuckin' necessary!

I handed her a box of blue Kleenex. It was empty.

That morning I shot the same shit, the same amount plus what I'd given him. I left the bathroom door unlocked. And it was good like God felt on the seventh day, real fuckin' good shit, but not enough. God, he'd be laughin', me too I guess, between a nod and a joke. It just wasn't my turn.

Three days hence and there's no sun left, only gray skies without no fuckin' tears. Jim's a stone in the mud, a sea of dead stones, another ghost. Buttkins, Henderson, Walsh, Casey fuckin' Jones! It's all screamin' out, out the back of my ungodly damned forsaken brain. Beep! It's over, over and again. Life's like war, its own consequential nightmare. I consoled his wife over stiff drinks, with a stiff dick, boned both her and her baby sister, but wouldn't stay the night. "You sleep with no one," as Myles put it, "or you might never wake the fuck up!" And me, I'd been sleeping with the enemy.

Swishhhhhh, splashing me up! These dead roads are all I'm about anymore. The hiss of traffic over wet pavement like the hiss, the hissing of a killer King snake. Jesus, I ain't never comin' back.

◆   ◆   ◆

The heat was coming up like it rises off in the distance, down the road like some oasis about to happen. I was soaked and free, freezing under a blanket of depravity and wantonness, alcohol and drugs seeping out of every pinprick, bits of metal from my leg. The war couldn't be stopped, and I was tired of trying.

"Jesus, I need some help here!"

My kidneys had rebounded. Doctor Sampson said I'd dodged a speeding bullet, it wasn't the first time. I told the nurse I wasn't John Doe 151, that she'd been an angel, and again like Lazarus I rose up from the tomb.

◆   ◆   ◆

4

"What Else Is Gone"

Other than Jesus, who stuck around for forty days, me and Lazarus are the only ones come back from the dead. What did he do with himself? Was he that much more inspired, capable of smelling the roses? What meaning, purpose had his return to life? Did he bring back messages from the dead? Drink your milk. Keep your house orderly. Beware of thieves in the night. Did he split town with Mary M. and start up a family? Or was his resurrection regifted like mine, damaged goods, abbreviated text, full of ifs? And if you could see my thoughts, minus dreams like a man missing limbs, without no face, blue lips impressed upon a blue palm, you might believe me. If you could put your finger here. Where the bullet, the button and the needle left its hole, where the bleeding starts and stops, over, over and again, you might understand. I am not like you! We are not of the same world. All that's left me here, out of necessity, is fixed to the page, all that's constant anymore, and what else is gone.

I had an idea about dying right here, at this very moment. Fuck this book! I could drink laundry detergent, blue bubbles. I like the smell, mountain breeze, the texture like smooth rolling hills. I've always been partial to blue, peaks, skyscapes, but gray anymore are these shortened days, my sunken eyes, baggy flesh. I'd drink it all up! It would clean me out, make me blue all over again.

And me, I just blew four and a half year's clean time on a three-day run. Don't know yet if I'm actually finished. Jesus, what's over and again hasn't stopped. What's really done? Who is it? Whose meaning eludes me like a face on blown currency, in God we trust, but it's Ben Franklin, Casey fuckin' Jones, Jimmy, Rodney's footprint on each hundred-dollar shot. Before this it was fifteen months, eight, six, nine, and the flashbacks, those blue gray days of panic, anxiety screamin'. And the doctors couldn't figure out why this dreadful fright? Where the fuck it came from, or how to stop it. I'd be hyperventilating, couldn't fuckin' breathe, in and out of emergency rooms, waiting benches, psych wards, pacing up and down corridors, don't cross the red line, and they'd give me a patch to smoke. I'd leave the hospital the worst for it only to return a few days later. Because, just because, knowing they couldn't fix me, but I'd nowhere else to go.

They'd be changing meds like revolving doors go round, and round, sometimes as many as five at a time like I was a spinning top, a wheel of misfortune. No, nothin' worked, try this, tried that, but no exit. Just a constant agitated gnawing at my innards, steam from a kettle like a fiery cauldron, milk to butter as if I were being churned to death, turned inside out. I'd have preferred war, rockets and mortars, intense combat to this desperate state of affairs. My insides imploding, and on the outside I couldn't fuckin' move. My only reprieve was sleep, but I'd wake harnessed like frictitious metals scraped atop fleeting pavement as if tightly strung from a busted-up gas line, shoot, shooting off in a flurry of sparks, about to ignite, blow! My cigarette pull it'd be drawn hard and long, my ash sucked hot and steep and consuming itself like me into billows of smoke, and rusty cough. Those mornings that were once upon a time the best of it, clear headed, alert and alive, were now the worst of times. Now I had the whole fuckin' day to endure, one, one shortened breath at a time before I'd get me my sleepy-time narcotic again.

I'd beg God to fix me, heal me, please! Went to church every day, ate the bread, meetings, more meetings, read the bigger than big book, all of it! What limited, simple life I lived was now insolvable. No, nothin' worked, stopped the gnashing of teeth. Not the alcohol, not the dope, but for shootin' coke, then my outsides were going as fast as my insides. In this way I was capable of doing some laundry, cutting the grass, I'd make the fuckin' bed.

The doctors, social workers, administrative pimps ran out of options, wanted me in a day-care center like a retard, to play word games, Bingo, listen to the radio, have lunch, share our drool. And the panic, it was all that was constant. Out of desperation I quit the system, stopped the meds, medicated my own self. Completed sentences, notebooks full, run-on sentences I'd left abbreviated, accumulated over the years, boxes full, a closet full of boxes. I wrote my way out. Wrote a fuckin' play.

It stopped! They didn't know how or why, but the panic subsided. What had seemed an eternity in damnable, hellish skins. A year or so later a doctor at another VA suggested it might have been a thyroid medicine they'd given me to enhance an already failing antidepressant. Fuck! It may have been the cause of all that fuckin' panic.

When I first got clean and sober, I put together almost nine years, med free. I'd put the war on the shelf, the back burner, and made no excuses anymore for picking up. But as it came to be, any crises or loss would send me catapulting back to Vietnam, and each time it occurred with greater severity than the previous episode. In the end I was all but overwhelmed, toppled over, caught up in flames, couldn't stop my crying all the time, or comprehend why the tears. Jesus, I couldn't fuckin' move.

I'll be fifty-six soon, and feel as if I've already gone the distance. These last four and a half years haven't given me a newfound freedom.

I'm still at war, can't seem to stop it. I've looked, but can't find Myles anywhere. I've never seen anyone again I'd served in Vietnam with, only these ghosts. I write alone, drive myself to meetings, eat alone, sleep alone, and shit myself. It's hard to leave the apartment, if I go to the store, needing supplies, food, clothing, I go early, or late at night to avoid the crowds. "If!" If I only had a life. No wife, lovers, there ain't even any possibilities. No hopes, only nightmares, no kids that I know of, guess there could be a few in Southeast Asia. My old sponsor Bill, the confrontational prick, who walks a spry health shake like gait like he had a celery stalk stuck up his ass, says I'm only feeling sorry for myself. He don't wanna read this book, doesn't like the title, says there ain't no ghosts. I'm not dead, is what he believes, I'm grandiose. "You's one lucky motherfucker!"

He's busy traveling the globe, investigating disasters, doing volunteer work, actually he's writing a book about trauma. He's never once tasted the blood! No, he's not swimming in a sea of brain matter, he's never even once traded places with anyone, and watched them fuckin' die! Doesn't know the "If!" of fucking it! He, and his kind just make my homecoming all that more difficult, virtually impossible.

Don't know who of my sober friends, if any I want to call. My kidneys hurt, double me up like Quasimodo. There's an anvillike weight knotting my chest, it won't straighten me out, but at least I can pee. I ain't goin' back to the hospital, dialysis is out of the equation, can't live like that. I'm old, too fuckin' old for this shit, smoked too many cigarettes. Yeah, I'm coughing up white phlegm, they say that's when you're close to done. My future, it's twenty years past, when I first got clean and sober, quit smoking, was busy doing push-ups. Or is it that I've never come back from the war?

I'd like to be that age again when life's problems could be held, comforted by a motherly embrace, but I'm too big, it's too late. I'm sitting here, this darkened corner of the room, behind my desk looking out against blackened picture-window glass, sliding glass doors. It's all black! Is there no one to call? "Hello God, it's only me, but I've got nothin' to say. Hey man, are there no stunningly beautiful gorgeous babes to make call your name out loud?" This furniture I've accumulated, these seats where no one sits, to straighten this, that, and again to make the bed as if it mattered anymore like the button and unbuttoning of shirts, besides, there's always another ashtray t' empty. One last cup t' wash. Another train whistle screamin' off in the distance. Those are my lips pressed up against the black glass. My black lips! And this is where we meet again my suckling ghost. And what else is gone.

This place ain't nowhere, no, nothin' but a glorified bunker! Everything you do believe, you do believe has a reason, but mine's unwilling. It's 10:00 P.M. Do you know where my children are? I move out, between, above and below the line, everything falls through like a ceiling does, like a boy without any windows. No one's waiting, no one's home, no one's expected anymore, it's too late, they've all left with someone else. But for these ghosts, waiting on me. "If!" *Rinnnng!* I don't answer it. It's only some asshole tryin' to sell me what? Who needs it! Jesus, there ain't no one here anymore, not even me feelin' sorry for you. It's been seven days, I should be finished, detoxed, should take a fucking break.

◆   ◆   ◆

"Judas!"

"I don't believe you!" He told the heckler amongst a jeering crowd, and turned to the Band, "Play it fuckin' loud!"

It's the same thing here, they don't wanna hear it, it's too fuckin' intense, too many *fucks* and *fuckin's*, too sad, too depressing. Too many exclamation points! Too electric! Told one friend I was gonna write a children's book, "Billy's Black Fuckin' Lunch Box!" He laughed, but insisted I should be doin' somethin' else, get me outta myself, some volunteer work. But I've volunteered enough. This is my job! And if you ain't pissin' at least a few people off it probably ain't worth sayin', Jesus, you know that better than anyone. And me, I'm gonna play it, play it fuckin' loud, cause, because it's the fucking truth!

"Vietnam wasn't for everyone," some fool whined, after I'd read the first chapter to a packed coffee house, got me a standing ovation. Vietnam wasn't for anyone, were my only thoughts, but it's fuckin' real. I don't believe you! You ain't so white on white motherfucker, and I ain't so black.

Ten days and I just had to have me another run. Went a little crazy, spilled my ginger ale, tore up the place, shredded three pair of shorts, backed up the toilet, used up all my towels, some shirts soaking up the flood. Banged my works down the kitchen drain with a hammer and some nails. Loaded full my last three sets, all the coke I'd left, leaving just a pinch of room for blood, needed to know it was all in vein. It was more than enough, plenty enough to kill any one man. I was ready for leaving. Wanted to clean up the mess, but didn't have the strength, besides, death ain't neat. Lay there naked in the bed as if on a cross wearing only a dead man's bloody head bandanna. Tied off on both arms using the same long-sleeved shirt, buttonless, shot it all at once like three wise men bearing gifts. Bloodied the sheets. Left no note, real suicides don't leave notes. I wasn't feelin' sorry for nothin', you're the thief! This just might be my only way home.

An hour earlier I'd labored the bed into a frenzied display, against its opposite, opposing wall, against and into shadows, neighboring windows, all the intimacy I'd left. Now I lay here, lay me down to sleep, wrong side up, staring out at that picture of a boy on a hillside without any glass. Years ago I'd retrieved it from the attic. Initially it had been my Godmother's, Aunt Marie's. How intrigued I'd been as a child, was the boy really asleep? Were the sheep off somewhere getting lost?

Truly I'd surrendered, truly it's over. I'd stopped sweating. A tranquility came over me, all the commotion ceased, faded away, as if to rest in peace. I was fearless anymore, seeing all along that death had been my only truth, yes, this dying, it will surely stop the noise.

And I saw in that picture like one, one branch of blue sky, God, God above the noise, the clouds, blue eyed, watchin' over the boy, looking out at me. "Not yet!" a voice said. I ate some bread, it was all I could stomach, piece by bit by piece until I fell asleep.

And again like Lazarus I'd been resurrected from the dead, meat from bread like wine into blood. But this time it's different, and the difference, "Jesus," it's invigorating ain't it! This being dead, it's better than killing, better than surviving bullets, mortars, fuckin' B-40s. Now I'd seen eternity's wings like chariots afire, all them whistles, rockets and trains like wind chimes culminating into one precise, enlightened crescendo like a halo rainin' down on me. And it's all fuckin' good! Now there's hope, this shit, it's only temporal. But first this book as if I'd been commanded, commissioned by God, clearly as one and one makes three. It's why I'm one, one lucky motherfucker! And this ghost on my tongue.

"If!" And if I look long enough into the black glass, there's another living room reflected there, as much alive as this one. A black doorway that leads to a black hole, a black screen like the black Dead Sea, where nothing grows. And all seems dead here, but for the Beast, who lives, eats, and sleeps with me.

"I'm hungry," it says.

"I'm food," and spread my arms like fishes and loaves of bread. "Swallow me up, and I'll turn you fuckin' blue!" There's that train whistle again, wrong side up. And all I do, do believe in anymore, is writing this down. It's how the words do find me now, make me right side up.

◆   ◆   ◆

"Forget the dead you've left they will not follow you." You're wrong, Bob! Dead wrong! I don't believe you! It ain't all over now, Baby Blue, not yet.

◆   ◆   ◆

5

"And So the War Ends"

The war never stops for some of us soldiers, but it ended for you back in 1975. Fifteen years long, some lost sons, husbands, fathers they never met, 58,000 plus on our side, and all for nothin'! Three million of them, but they got what they believed in, their independence. You can't put no bodily price tag on that, and as they saw it they would have continued the fight no matter the cost. We knew we'd lost after the Tet Offensive of '68, but made this half-assed asinine attempt to pull out with honor, seven more years, and how many more lives spent? All for nothin'! Me, I was there in '69, '70, what made no difference in the outcome of the war, but did manage to ruin my life.

We were stopping the spread of communism, yeah, right! "Ask not what your country can do for you," I ate that bullshit up like a starving schoolboy with a drunk for a dad. "But what you can do for your country," I needed somethin' to believe in. And for some the war it never existed, or it'd been partially obscured, unreal, over there, far off somewhere over the fuckin' rainbow, not in Kansas anymore, but a foreign distant other world, a jungle land you'd never heard of. Sure, it'd been photographed, televised, but those channels you repeatedly skipped over, you wouldn't touch it, you were ill informed, unaffected.

Some heartfelt activists, revolutionaries, the antiwar movement, those who'd championed the good fight were now seemingly idle, what was a girl like Jane to do? A sense of believing, a oneness in stride had been lost without the meaningfulness of rallies, marches, and demonstrations. Protest songs became obsolete, all we'd left to sing about anymore was love, trucks, trains, highways, and an occasional oil spill.

And others had been murdered in Ohio, some were beaten with sticks, fists, gassed in Chicago, throughout the land. But all for somethin'! Cops were pigs anymore, but could now go back to being policemen. And My Lai, it was political fodder, media hype, a scapegoat for what I saw every fuckin' day. And who's the enemy here? I don't want to be the one. Jesus, what a fuckin' mess this entire war had been.

Oh well, most of you thought, we made a few mistakes, lost a war we shouldn't have fought, or didn't fight it good enough, but now that it's over let's forget about it. Let's all mend our differences, be friends, and just pretend like it never happened. And you tucked it away, as far away as you could put it, stuffed it, the likes of me into a closet like an urn full of ashes, a belly full of ghosts, abbreviated text, intrusive thoughts, run-on sentences. A fuckin' bunker full of secrets like a dead man in a box, still breathing.

We too tried to forget, kept our mouths shut, said nothin', no nothin', about the war, grew our hair long and tried to fit in, to be a part of. Some went to work, the post office was hiring, still others couldn't find work, many went to prison. Me, I went back to school on the GI Bill, learned somethin', got me a degree in literature, but said nothin', no nothin' until now.

And what have you learned? The Vietcong are now called "insurgents." Another fuckin' enemy undercover, and you don't know who it is. Now you've got Abu Ghraib, we killed our prisoners, took no photographs. And again, it's happening again, you can't win this war! My nephew just out of high school went off and joined the Marines. I said all that I could, but couldn't stop 'im. It all sounds too familiar.

◆   ◆   ◆

I'd be leaning against the wall, holding me up, under dark glasses, waiting, just waiting for the classroom across the hall to empty out, so I'd be the first inside, get me a good seat against the back wall. I needed to be in a corner, have one side covered, my ass protected, and everything in front of me at all times. Some strange girl would pass, barely out of high school, inquisitively, she'd ask, "How come you never smile?" I said nothin'. I was unaware I wasn't smiling, how depressed and sad I really was. I'd be stoned all the time, had a war in my head I was tryin' to suppress.

"If!" If she only knew, but there was no one to tell about it, no one had a fuckin' clue who I really was, what I'd seen and done. Even the VFW wanted nothin' to do with us, said Vietnam wasn't a war, but a conflict. It was fine with me, fuck them! I'd had my fill, didn't wanna be joining anything anymore.

I turned in this paper I'd written as class was letting out, Ms. Wright requested I keep my pessimism to myself and out of her classroom. I didn't understand, must have been somethin' I said. All I remember about the paper was comparing James Dean in *Rebel Without a Cause*, with Robert De Niro in *Taxi Driver*. Somethin' about the evolution of the American hero from a bad-mannered, rebellious adolescent into an ill-tempered, destructive psychopath. I got nervous, skipped a few classes after that, but when I did go back she sincerely apologized. I had no idea why, why she said what she did in the first place. I got an A, she might have been afraid of me. Me, no, wouldn't hurt nobody, but where the fuck was I? Guess I wasn't so much in school, this serene quietlike country setting, as sitting on the spare tire of an open gun jeep manning an M-60 machine gun, patrolling a mountain side, shootin' up a dirt road, making ripples in a rivers bed, pounding back flesh. Jesus, I still had metal leaking out my leg.

I'd read *Nausea*, *The Stranger*, *The Idiot*, Victor Hugo, Balzac, *Native Son*, Kafka, Bradford, *Junky*, Rilke, *The Bell Jar*, T. S. Eliot, *Waiting for Godot*, Leroi Jones, Charles Bukowski, and Blake's *The Marriage of Heaven and Hell*, I knew something about hell! Found myself walking through village huts, abbreviated steps, quietlike, identifying shadows, my M-16 rifle tightly strapped across my forearm, set on fully automatic, ready to blast the fuck off. She said somethin' in Vietnamese I didn't understand, reached too quickly for something under her blanket. Told her to stop, repeated myself, I couldn't see all that well. But she didn't stop, no, maybe she didn't understand me. What I thought was a weapon was only her baby, only a baby. Fuck! Fuck! Fuck!

Professor Patterson summoned me back to attention, wanted to know what I'd thought of John Berryman's poetry. "I like it, but he's a dead man. Can't be writin' the shit he's writing, Mr. Bones, Henry, them *Dream Songs* and expect to survive himself." A short time later Berryman jumped off a bridge, all smiles, waving goodbye.

◆   ◆   ◆

Fifteen years since I'd left Vietnam, ten years after the war ended with the fall of Saigon, and the city's given us a parade. I'm watchin' it on TV like some of you had viewed the war, from a soft chair. Can't do no crowds. I'm cryin', maybe you're cryin' some too, but there's nothin' to cheer about. We'd lost! Yeah, this parade, it's a nice gesture, real sweet, but just too fuckin' late. Still I'm watchin' the TV real close, lookin' for someone, anyone I might recognize, but I don't see no one I know.

"Welcome home," hey, you've finally said it. Now you can put away your guilt, rest easy, good citizens, and forget we ever existed. Other than good old Bones, family members, a few close friends, it's been mostly what we've told each other.

"Welcome home," and the shaking of hands like unwanted guests, desperate to believe, reassure ourselves, "Jesus!" We actually belong here. But we were the ones who left, shouldn't we have been welcomed home by those who stayed behind? Couldn't it have been a little sooner?

Ten years home from the war, I was drunk at the local bar, playin' pinball with a young sailor home on leave. He'd read all the war books, was a fuckin' historian, and when he caught wind I'd been in Vietnam he bought me a drink. His Uncle Joe had been in da Nam, was never the same after that, quietlike, and kept to himself, had blown his fuckin' head off just six months ago. It was the first and last time anybody ever bought me a drink because I'd been in Vietnam. All us soldiers ever really had was each other, and that connection was weak at best being that we came and left alone, like I said, it was an individual war. I've searched real hard, keep tryin', still, I've never seen anyone again I'd been in Vietnam with, but for these ghosts. Is there no one left here to validate these truths?

I'd gone back to my parents home, hadn't been seen or heard from in five years. I'd run out of roads, places to stay, women to care for me, I was unemployable, wasted, strung out, and needed help somethin' bad. I'd nowhere else to go. During my absence my dad had gotten sober, a fuckin' miracle I'd thought, a real dad, and for the first time in my life I wanted to be like him. Where's my daisy-flowered bathing cap?

I was allowed a temporary stay under the condition I seek treatment. I'd called the VA hospital and was waiting on a screening to determine my eligibility, my willingness to change, and for a bed to become available. Seems there was an abundance of junkies just lookin' to get out from the cold, three hots and a cot, and to lessen their habits, so they didn't need so much to get high anymore.

My old mattress was still on the floor, the walls were bare and still needed more than paint. My old dresser had been replaced for an older beat-up one. Good old Bones had died long ago of old age. My sisters were nurses, John a counselor, Billy a mailman. They'd all left home, were married now with children. I'd missed two weddings and two babies being born. Everyone had grown up but me, I was fuckin' nine-teen, spun myself round and round, and at thirty-five was still a war-crazed adolescent.

I was married once, a few years back, it lasted four months. She went without my knowing, got some help, and stopped enabling me. In turn I lost everything. She also came to terms with her sexuality, admitted she was a lesbian. I've always been attracted to strong, petite women who act manly. She wasn't so petite, but farted like a truck driver. Later I'd jokingly say, "Once you've had the best why have the rest." After me women either changed their sexual preference or married the next guy they met.

Bette was a good person, but there was no real love. I only needed a caretaker, and she a sick patient to care for. In one of my attempts to get straight she'd gone and sized me up. "It must have been the dope all along, you're really not that interesting." She wouldn't have sex with me anymore. Once she left I watched it all disappear——appliances, fur-niture, the window gates, the phone, the fuckin' electricity, even the suit I was married in. I got me a roommate, but still couldn't pay my half the rent. Without her I'd lost all pretense of responsibility. Didn't know who I was, but alas a fuckin' junkie.

Waiting to hear from the hospital I took a ride one night, out of boredom, curiosity I guess, went back to the airport lookin' for Elijah, but he'd gone off and died a few years earlier, had a heart attack while on the job.

◆   ◆   ◆

Don't know if I'll finish this book. I'm tired, this same old shit as if it mattered anymore, or less. They don't wanna hear it, as if I had a fuckin' choice. I don't want to be the one, the last dead soldier left alive. Yeah, I'd like to be an unmarked page like one, one blue branch of sky, a ribbon for your hair. I miss Rodney, Myles, and all the rest of me I could have been.

◆   ◆   ◆

Jocko, whose real name was Carmen, was a big white guy who copped his dope in Harlem late at night. He'd be wearing jungle fatigues, combat boots, and had a .45 tucked under his belt. He came home from the war a junkie. Me too, I'd go into bad places, abandoned buildings like bomb-smeared landscapes. Once across Avenue C I'd be in the red zone, the adrenaline would start pumpin', that, driving fast and sticking a needle in my arm were all that made me feel alive anymore. I needed the threat of impending death like a long-distance runner needs a finishing line. Again, over and again, might this be my last shot? Ring a few bells, knock me off my feet.

We were in this TC, therapeutic community, a ninety-day program to make us not junkies anymore. We had this group on Thursdays where one of us would be put on the hot seat, made to sit in the middle of the circle, and be bombarded with questions from all fronts. Jocko was fending off everyone, all confrontational advances, he was unaffected like he was stone-cold-fortified numb. He didn't care that he stole from his wife, picked up her paycheck at the hospital where she worked as a nurse, and shot it up. Went back to her employer, said the check blew out the car window, had them issue another one, and shot that one up too. Yeah, he stole his mother's jewelry, her wedding ring, silverware, TV, rent money. "So what," was all he could say.

Just a few days ago he'd been pulled over by a cop, no sweat, he thought, having shot the last of a bundle just minutes ago. He felt good, real good about himself, above the fuckin' law. The cop said somethin' about him usin' dope. "No Sir, not me," he replied, his baby blues pinned to the back of his brain. The cop looked straight through them dead pools, them reservoirs of deceit.

"So why all them empty heroin bags stuck to the side of your vehicle?" It'd been raining, and what he thought he'd thrown away, out the fuckin' window, had adhered to the side of his jeep.

"Jesus," was all he said. Jocko got busted, the courts had ordered him here, but far as he was concerned it was the fuckin' rain's fault. Jocko didn't give a shit about nothin'! No nothin', until someone asked him about his first kill. A drastic change came over him, his face lost all color, bleached bone white, he trembled, not just his legs but all over, his words became ever so tearful. He'd been standing over a dead gook he'd shot in the head, the bullet came out the back of his brain, you know the colors, the pink, and blue, and gray of it. Gooks bleed just like us, look the same on the inside.

Jocko started crying, his sergeant approached, "Mother fuckin' bull's-eye!" he shrieked. Noticed Carmen's tears, and smacked him across the face. "Hey Jocko, you'd better get used to it." He did, became a collector of ears, wore a fuckin' necklace. Jocko got so upset at one point he had to rush off from the confines of the circle and go fuckin' puke.

That night we were sitting around the day room, just shootin' the shit. Jocko started telling this story about a sniper he'd shot. The fucker was up in a tree, had killed five of his buddies. Jocko had shot him in the lung, a gaping wound. The remainder of the story he told in third person, but we all suspected he was talkin' about himself. "My friend came up, dropped his pants and started fuckin' the corpse in the lung, in the hole, in the fuckin' wound, he'd be fuckin' him, and fuckin' 'im, just be fuckin' 'im!" Jocko got so excited, animatedlike that he got up from his seat, arms swinging, fists poundin' at air, "and he be fuckin' 'im like crazy!" he bellowed. And smack, right there before our fuckin' eyes, under tight-fitting fatigues was a giant, screaming, throbbing hard on. He'd fuckin' gone and popped bone!

"Jesus!" How fucked up can one guy get?

This place had a bunch of fuckin' stupid rules. Once I had to wear a pacifier around my neck because I'd supposedly acted like a baby, had to listen to Ted the head counselor scream at me, tell me how fuckin' small and insignificant I actually was, and couldn't say nothin' back. Some were made to carry around embarrassin' signs, labeling themselves as junkies and losers. Writing assignments were given out like malaria pills on a hot swampy jungle trod, for the slightest infraction like forgetting to sign out, an unbuttoned shirt, or a sloppily made bed. Everybody was constantly tellin' everybody else, "Pull up," which meant change your behavior ASAP. The dopers were leading the dopes, and you couldn't do nothin', even doin' nothin' and you'd be confronted, accused of havin' a hidden agenda.

There were these Cardinal rules—no drugs, no sex, no stealing, no violence or threats of any kind, a violation of any one of these and you were kicked out, no questions asked. "Who's shootin' dope in my house?" It was Ted's favorite fuckin' line. The next day Jocko brought an apple with him back from the mess hall, an apple he was entitled to, and was booted out for stealing, carted off to fuckin' jail. He'd be cryin'. Jesus, a fuckin' apple!

Me, I lasted three more days. I'd said somethin', and some asshole told me, "Pull up."

I grabbed my crotch and told 'im, "Pull up on this!" That was it, I was thrown the fuck out. But best be sure, I was real fuckin' happy about it.

◆   ◆   ◆

I'd beat myself up enough, didn't need anyone doin' it for me. Had enough guilt and shame, sinned enough to be my own religion. My dad he'd gone to AA, thought I'd give it a shot. I immersed myself in the program, they were warm, welcoming, gentle. I'd found a home in church basements, meetings and more meetings, it worked, got me clean and sober. Fifteen years since I'd left the war, and I was finally coming back to life. I turned off the TV, didn't need no fuckin' parade, told the folks, "I'm goin' out to a meeting." I'm a survivor, the war, I thought, it's over.

◆   ◆   ◆

6

"Redemption on the Lam"

And when He had said these things, He cried out with a loud voice, "Lazarus, come forth." He who had died came forth, bound hand and foot with wrappings; and his face was wrapped around with a cloth. Jesus said to them, "Unbind him, and let him go." (John 11 : 43,44)

◆　　　◆　　　◆

Here I am between chapters like lampposts, mile markers on a deserted stretch of country road, beware of sheep crossing. I am not the prodigal son but the wounds and sores of Lazarus for a dog to lick, yes, crumbs from your table, but eternity will be in the bosom of Abraham. And in the end you'll have wished, "If!" If only you'd listened.

It's the last day of November 2005, the back wood is bare, no leaves left, but waiting on the snows. There are no birds singing, no sun, but overcast skies without the tears. It does heighten the colors though in a subdued fashionable manner, more alive than dead. I've spent the last twenty-one years in and around the program, about sixteen of those years clean and sober, just not continuously. It's kept me a survivor. I have me, myself today, and this book I'm writing. That's it!

"I don't know where I'm going, how it ends, just where I've been," said the dead man to the Beast. I splash some water on my face, but still come back orange. Ain't no one else here. Jesus, it's only me but for these ghosts intruding upon my thoughts, you know, the pink, and blue, and gray of it. I have a new used pen, a cramped right hand, a crumpled sheet of blank page. I write the next word. These damaged goods are all that's left me here, unbound.

◆   ◆   ◆

I spent the first two years of recovery living with my parents. They were very good to me, generous, supportive of my doings. It was also an opportunity to heal old wounds, get to know each other again, anew. My first ninety days I couldn't work, had trouble getting out of bed, couldn't fuckin' move, couldn't sleep, but did go to a lot of meetings. I'd go early, set up tables and chairs, leave late, break it all down, clean the coffee pot. I didn't have to think if I kept moving. I'd spend hours at the diner with my sponsor, my ride, and a booth full of sobriety. All I wanted, could afford was a cup of tea, but I listened, learned somethin'. I'd wasted years getting high, it was all I knew, hadn't a fuckin' clue how not to. They taught me HOW. An acronym for Honest, Open, and Willing, and I was all of that.

My dad dropped me off at a meeting one night five miles from home, told me to find my own way back. It was a great thing he did, I was forced to ask for help. It was only my third meeting, I knew no one. Some elderly gentleman was giving me a ride, a retired liquor salesman who, when he got sober, his newly found AA friends carried out on a stretcher, out from his basement, seventeen cases of twelve-year-old scotch. "It was either the booze, or me," he'd say, "gonna be carted off on that stretcher." Seems EMS workers had been to his house many times before, and on one occasion, a false alarm, they'd forgotten their gurney. Bob believed they'd done it purposely in preparation for his final exit.

I told Bob I was having trouble with the God aspect of the program. He reached into the back seat and handed me a big book, AA's general text, and told me to read the chapter to the agnostics. I did, it was comforting, I could wrap myself around a creative intelligence. The second step was also very gentle, I could use the group as a whole, as a power greater than myself. In the beginning all I could read was a sentence or two before my thoughts sifted off into space like particles, junk collectibles. I'd have to read it over, the same bad prose over, and again. I read a little each day, a bit more the next. My first six months all I'd read was AA literature, books, pamphlets, I read it all.

I got a job as a waiter. I'd been around the food business for years, had countless short-lived experiences, from hawking football games as a kid, pizza parlors, delis, finer restaurants—that, liquor stores, and bars had been the mainstay of my employment. One of my best friends, Len Kocis, who I renamed Cy, fell into a superb opportunity, doing food and beverage for backstage crews and rock bands. We did quality foods prepared fresh, and had at our disposal the best of drugs, top-shelf booze, wines, and champagnes. It was Cy and I'd and James. Sounds almost biblical, it's not. Cy also employed a host of rising starlets, the Firm Ms. Fern, Loretta the Sweater Petter, and Quaaludia Zits. The only time I ever saw her move with any conviction was when I'd called her a cunt, and she chased me about the room with a failed tray of Crab Louie. And who could forget the youngster, Bubba, who later insisted on being called by his real name, Robert, but he remained the Bubbster. Bubba aspired to be like me and James, and also became a junkie. Appropriately, the business was affectionately known as "Kitchen Cy Kocis."

We'd start the day with a fat joint, a few lines, and a bottle of Cristal. Cy and James did the cooking, others prep. As pantry chef I knew where everything was, like I'd always had to since the war, that and every sound I needed to identify. I also took care of the dressing rooms. There's another story here, but not for this book. I'm not the one to tell it. I worked part time with Cy for ten years, lived in his house as much. A good friend, he'd always bail me out, many times in the middle of the night, put me up when I was on the lam. Once I helped him move, and stayed for two years.

Cy was a heavy hitter, but never lived above the line. Not like me and James, and so many others on the backstage circuit. He acknowledged I had a problem, others denied it, so as not to look at themselves. He was supportive, is still to this day. The rock-and-roll lifestyle was over, too great a temptation for me anymore. Besides being a great chef and a fifth-degree black belt, Cy's a chiropractor today, has a loving wife and three kids. He's one of the most caring and tolerant of persons, of anyone I've ever met. Cy can break 'em, fix 'em, and feed 'em. He's a happy man.

That waiter job didn't last too long, about six months. One weekend, despite the threats, I just had to go to New Orleans to act in a friend's movie. I'd taken some graduate courses in film, didn't finish, blew a half-tuition scholarship, but periodically I'd get me some acting work. Besides, I had to be in all Jim's movies. I got fired! But I found me another job as an assistant counselor in an adolescent rehab. I stayed there about a year, the money was shit, couldn't live on it even living with my parents, but I liked working with the kids, helped a few, and it kept me sober. There were a handful of old friends I sought out, James included, helped them help themselves get clean and sober. Bubba never made it, went to prison.

Two years into recovery I moved back to the city. It's where I'd gone to grad school years prior, was at the core of my bottom. I'd left it all to get clean. I found me a tiny room in a boardinghouse in the East Village, it was smaller than a bunker. My futon took up the width of the room, I'd have to roll it up to walk, but I had a sink to pee in and a window to write out of. The walls were bruised and lumpy as if beaten with a sledge, I'd almost nothin' to hang in the small walled-in closet, and was still living out of a duffle bag. The landlord was in the program, most of his tenants were in early recovery, between apartments, they'd stay a few months, get back on their feet, and be gone. Me, I stayed six years. It's the longest I've ever lived in any one place.

After two interviews I got the job I'd prayed for as a gym teacher in a private boys' school. It was all in sobriety I'd ever asked of God, other than to live each day clean and sober. What seemed like a natural progression, I'd still be working with teens, and it was enough money to live on. Three weeks later, I reported for my first day of work. The head coach had been forced to rehire someone he didn't like, "I'm overstaffed," that's what he said. I got fired before I even started. Couldn't help but think there was some other reason, the way the principal whispered somethin' in his ear, stared me down as he left the room. Fuck! I was broke, hadn't been looking, and now I was out of work.

I found myself teetering, walking the streets looking for a job, spent days, weeks, couldn't find one. Felt as if I'd just come back from the war, walked out of the jungle, didn't fit, didn't belong here like all I deserved was to be dead like all good soldiers had died tryin' to be good. Where the fuck is Myles? I've got a hole in my soul.

I wandered out of desperation into a Vets center, a tiny office on the ground floor of a grubby hotel. A hole in the wall with one counselor, seated in a rickety chair behind a splintering desk. It didn't fuckin' matter, I so badly needed to talk to someone. "If!" Rockets, mortars, explosions all around me. Bounce, fuckin' bouncin' Betty! The enemy was everywhere. Jesus, "Help!"

And it was as if I'd fallen into grace, "a sound indeed to patchhhh it!" A lighting production company had called just an hour ago, and the boss man was looking to hire some Vietnam vets. He told me later,

"You guys deserve a break." So I'd found me a job, and started therapy on a weekly basis.

The shop foreman was a nice guy, the job sucked, but it was a job. I worked the loading dock, a ground-floor tunnel that ran the width of a city block. Nothin' but truck fumes, and lots of heavy lifting, packing lights, poles, dimming boards, amp racks, and tons of fuckin' cable. It was free, freezing cold, and the wind whipped itself about, wrapped around the sweat of cloth and sent chills to the fuckin' bone.

After the heat of the war my blood had thinned, even on a hot summer's day the ocean was too damn cold, this was hell in an ice box. God's answer to my fuckin' prayers. The shop foreman didn't mind if I missed one or two days of work a week, most weeks I had to. He'd send anyone with a drinking or drug problem to come and see me, or would ask my advice. One vet who got hired when I did was fired for repeatedly showing up drunk. He didn't wanna hear it, and almost killed someone hurling a rack of lamps into a truck. A danger to himself and others, "If!" If we were in the bush I woulda shot him. I made just enough money to live on, and kept that job until I found another.

Therapy was no real treat. I told my story from beginning to end without any reprieve. Six months later there was a changing of the guard. Ms. Ann took the helm, moved the office uptown, into a real office space, with pictures on the wall, new desks, and swivel chairs. A handful of counselors came on board, even a receptionist. Charlie made the coffee, watered the plants, always in jungle fatigues and a faded boonie hat, I don't think he ever left the place. Again I repeated my story for Ann, but this time it only made things worse. I felt stuck, overwhelmed, between the pink, and blue, and gray of it. But I didn't wanna use, kept the focus on survival, one fuckin' day at a time. I continued therapy for the next five years, adding a weekly group session to the mix.

I found me another job, Sophia's, a rat's nest of a bar on Fifth Street, between A and B. It kept me warm during winter months, smoke filled, but better than trucks, and the money, it was twice as good. Dollar mugs of draft, shots, a few mixed drinks, but no fuckin' martinis here, you'd be in the wrong place. They'd be three deep at the bar, rude, obnoxious, unequivocal dirt bags, but they tipped well. And me the conductor, one who orchestrates it all, the cunning, quick-witted ungracious barkeep, who told bad jokes. The floor it was concrete, had long ago been painted red, and since gone black. Chairs were broken, kept breaking, tables were slanted, made right with handfuls of coasters. The pool table scuffed, balls would turn up missing, I'd a drawer full of replacements. Too many fights, and an easy access weapon, more Q's were broken than functioned. And the bathroom a vomiting trough, full of empty heroin bags and misshot urine, the toilet was forever backing up. Still, it was a great job. I'd work three days a week, and could live on it, acting work, a cash bonus. The boss, he was a good guy, fair-minded, and I'd the freedom to take a day off whenever I got a part. I kept that job five years, until I stopped working altogether.

◆   ◆   ◆

My desk had been cut from a door window, a heavy board I'd placed on a night table, it worked, gave me the space I needed. I sat facing the wall. Between the lines I'd gaze to my right looking out at the street and neighboring tenements. It was all alive out there, how it really is, life outside the bunker.

◆   ◆   ◆

So this is as good as it gets, what seems like paradise. I'm above ground, and nobody's shootin' at me. Again, I don't know if I'll finish, if there's an ending to this book. I've spent my days writing my way out, to go splat in the dark to the pavement like all the rest, all the good soldiers.

A precautionary note: Yeah, I'm sorry for my mom. I've got one, one last cup. And I do, do believe it's my turn comin'. You've all lived too long expecting me to live a little longer. I'm tired, and the sun is going out. Soon, it will be all black. And "If!" If the blind might see, I might see you there.

◆   ◆   ◆

7

"Heaven"

I'm not really here, but a ghost anymore.

◆   ◆   ◆

The family directly across the street in a three-story building similar to the one I lived in, had two girls, a mom and a dad, it was a loving, happy family. Periodically the wife, the mother she'd leave for a few days, she'd be in uniform, wheeling an overnight bag. She was an airline hostess. I don't know what the father, the husband did, but he'd rush out early mornin' with bags of trash, race to beat the garbage truck bombarding up the street. He'd be barefoot, and would always win. When his wife returned there'd be cause for celebration.

My big window had a thousand-window view. I could see into the lives of others, without a word or touch. I was safe, protected, behind the glass, out of range. Confined to the page as if it were a bridegroom, between the lines, a reckless abandoned thief, yet no feelings at risk. "If." As if looking down from heaven. At the fire hydrant across the street kids would play in the spray, junkies would park and do a shot, having copped two blocks east. Up here I could deal with the contradictions, write it all down, fill in the blanks, without no fuckin' consequences. I remained unaffected, deadlike, but more alive than I'd ever been. And the most elegant of dog walkers would stop and pick up their dog's shit, that warm, soft, gushy feeling bonded them forever with their pet. It made me feel good. Up here I was King, bunker bound, "Tied to this heart by the King's chain." Jesus, and I knew which side of the cross I was on.

I imagined the father, the husband was a great artist, a composer of beautiful symphonies, and didn't like wearing shoes. The building to his left, my right, had five stories, each apartment three large windows. The woman of the middle, she'd hanging plants for curtains. We'd show each other our nakedness, a six-year romance, and we never spoke. She got pregnant, the guy must have split. I watched her belly grow, her tits get big. She was a joy to behold. And a son was born. It's the longest realationship I've ever known.

Hells Angels lived down the block. They'd be the ones who turned the fire hydrant on and off, guarded the street, kept it free of crime, and sold to the man the shit he sold to the junkie. We were an incestuous lot.

I'd go to work, work out, go to meetings, watch, write it all down. The old gray woman who lived on the ground floor, she never left her window, but sat in the memory of a life gone by. Bye, bye, she'd wave to those who passed like a child first learns how to say goodbye. Somethin' I'd never learned, or just forgot how to. Now it seems I get separation anxiety when the toilet paper runs out. Like me, most of her good friends had left her here. Again, over and again she might ask herself, is God ever this lonely?

A lesbian couple on the second floor paraded in the shadows of thread count, what might have been lace were curtains torn from bed sheets, as if spread across the sky, the social divide. We do agree that no one needs to know, who wouldn't understand.

And the woman at the top stands tall at her window in a bath towel, and clothlike turban like me no one's floor is her ceiling. Her deadbeat boyfriend, a gigolo, brought home another, and another, while she was away. She found out, and kicked him out. Hooray! Three cheers for the woman at the top! Now we both live alone.

◆   ◆   ◆

All my relationships were short lived, one-night stands, but were never meant to be that way. I'd spend some time, get to know someone, but once I'd slept with them I'd be gone. It's how it was, had to be in da Nam. I'd never spend the night.

◆   ◆   ◆

I'd gone first, it was my first time, she didn't have a name, might have been the enemy. Myles was busy humpin' away, pants and groans. There was a rustling outside the shack, voices, footsteps, moving closer. In a whisper, "Myles, there's somebody out there." There was no way of stopping Myles. The room had one window, no glass, clad with a dish towel, it moved. "Myles, Myles." He was on the verge of orgasm, trying to be quiet about it. I'd my .45, and his, out and ready, a two-pistoled cowboy, but I didn't know what to do next. Was it a friend or foe? A dim flashlight hit one corner, moved slowly across the room and stopped to rest on Myles black ass pounding away like a jackhammer. I couldn't shoot, they'd have to shoot first. Fortunately it was her uncle, a friend of his, they'd been out on patrol. Nobody got killed. Myles saw the woman a few days later, her husband found out, her face was all bruised, she'd been beaten up.

◆   ◆   ◆

I met her at a meeting, we had coffee after and talked through the night. A week later we watched a silent movie over at her place, *The*

Passions of Joan of Arc. We lay on her bed, did nothin', didn't even kiss, then she left for Paris. A year's study abroad, graduate courses in film criticism. We fell in love through the mail, letters became love letters. She sent me a black-and-white photograph, a self-portrait standing at the kitchen table in a striped bathrobe, long flowing curls showering down around her shoulders and breasts. When she returned the relationship lasted but a month. She got pregnant, had an abortion. It was me who couldn't do it, the distance worked, but nothin', no nothin' got too close. Didn't know it at the time, but I'd lost too much already.

Kept thinking someone would change me, love might fix me, but I remained fearful, cold, numb, distant, aloof. There were countless women, over, over and again, and always the same. They were all named Bette, bouncin' fuckin' Betty! Once I was at a meeting of forty people, and six of the women I'd slept with. Jesus! But up here I can't hurt no one, there are no words, no touching, there ain't no tears in heaven.

Charlie had the six of us, the whole group crying. Ann took a tissue from her purse, dabbed at her eyes and cheeks. Charlie had gotten in an argument with his best friend, Mickey, the mess cook, yeah, somethin' stupid. They'd spent almost the entire year living in the same tent, they'd been each other's solace, confidant's like blood brothers. Charlie left in a huff, an hour later he realized he was wrong, and went back to apologize. The tent had been hit, rocketed, and Charlie's friend Mickey was dead.

Just last week he'd seen in the paper a homeless man had died under the bridge. Charlie knew the guy was a vet, he'd seen him before panhandlin' the streets. Charlie contacted the proper authorities, got the guy a military burial. It was his way of making amends to Mickey. Now there's two more good soldiers smilin' down from heaven. Charlie's made his peace, and the pieces fit together again. Charlie's a whole man.

I knew her from the bar, then one day she showed up at a meeting. Didn't need the program for herself, was just being supportive, accompanying her friend. She stayed, got sober, her friend didn't. I had five years at the time, should have known better. This would be a first for me in sobriety, this relationship would break my fuckin' heart. It was on and off for about eight months, it was my fault, all the stops and starts. More than once I hurt her feelings. "Fuck you!" was the last thing she said, she only hated me anymore. And I really did love her, realized how much, but it was too fuckin' late.

I took the next year and a half off without any girlfriends, I'd been wounded, banged up, didn't wanna play anymore. The window was my only way out, my safe haven. I'd work at the bar, an occasional film part, worked out, and kept busy writing. The woman of the middle was breast-feeding her son, sometimes she'd squirt off a shot or two my way, I'd squirt back. One early mornin' a car double-parked alongside hers, this guy got out from the passenger seat and smashed her car window with a wrench. The old gray woman was still asleep, it was up to me to be a fuckin' angel like I was Artaud, the sympathetic monk to Joan's plight. I called the police, the guy looked up, saw me on the phone, knew what the fuck was goin' down, and split. They sped off, but not before I'd given the cops their license-plate number. Man, was she pissed when she saw all that broken glass. The police, they ran the plate, it seems the car they were driving had been reported stolen. I never did give my name, it didn't seem to matter, all that seemed important was keeping heaven in its place.

The last film I made in film school I'd shown to Nicolas Ray, he said I needed to make another film as soon as possible. It was the last film I ever made. Theater seemed more accessible, a cheaper way to get my work produced. I wrote a one-act play, "Open Mike" (a contemporary Western play with a side of baseball), an environmental piece to be performed in the bar. It was about a dysfunctional group of cowboys and cowgirls, and Pete Rose was the barkeep. Later it was moved to a theater in Soho.

She invited me to join her and some friends for coffee after a meeting. It was the first time we spoke, I'd seen her around, but never paid her much attention. We became part of the same crowd that hung out after meetings. And one night as it just happened it was only the two of us in the resturant. A week later we were sitting in the park, she was wearing a white T-shirt and jeans, not her usual skirt. I hadn't been looking, but at that moment I realized my attraction to her, her nipples were hard, we became more than just friends.

This relationship I'd done right, fell in love, and didn't waver. She was the one pulling and pushing, sucked me in, then blew me away. It lasted about nine months, she dumped me. Couldn't make up her mind, came back twice, and did it again. Again the war came crashing back, but worse than ever before. Hell's bells, and heaven was over, Jesus, I couldn't stop cryin'. I knew it wasn't about her, but more about Rodney, a head full of noise, and what losses I couldn't seem to comprehend. I'd be out at a restaurant, dinner with the family, anywhere, and the tears would come, sorrow and sadness would overwhelm me.

I wrote a one-act play about the war, this guy in a basement apartment, and the noise in his head. I thought I might write my way out. I haven't stopped writing this noise ever since, tryin' to make sense of a meaningless war. There were days I couldn't go to work, never missed work before, couldn't work out, couldn't read, some days I couldn't fuckin' write. I became less and less functional. Ann, my counselor and her peers kept suggesting, felt strongly that I needed to be on medication. I resisted, I'd done eight years without it. This too shall pass, I thought, God won't give me more than I can handle, but He did.

We had a special group on healing, it was attended by a former Vietcong soldier, and taped for a Sunday-morning news show. I didn't believe him, he'd lost friends, loved ones, but his touring the country was more about having trade sanctions lifted. I used the opportunity to make amends for my participation in the war. My apology was broadcast nationwide, but what worked for Charlie didn't work for me.

They told Charlie he couldn't make the coffee, or water the plants anymore, he couldn't hang out at the vets center all the time, he needed to have a life, find a real job, go home. Two weeks later he fuckin' hung himself. "If!" Another good soldier gone to heaven. After eight months of cryin', I acquiesced to the idea of medication.

I had to leave the fuckin' city, too much noise, traffic, confusion, all these sounds I could no longer distinguish between, like it was all incoming anymore. I was working only one day a week, had a small part in the film *Trees Lounge*, it was my last acting job. I waved goodbye to all my good neighbors, blew a kiss to the woman of the middle, and moved back in with my parents. Heaven, it had been short lived, it had been a lie.

◆   ◆   ◆

8

"Knots"

Knots are stillborn out from the noise, traffic stalled, still, stuck, lost the fuckin' directions, what was it that you're so late for? Potholes, button-holes, bullet holes and no fish, that one just fell the fuck off! Jesus, you can't take it with you, can't be the whole thing again, me too, I don't need to guess, rain, or is it hailin' bricks? Frogs everywhere, belly up, slick like an avalanche, the screams, yeah, I heard em' too, saw the cloud, burnin', crackle, pop like eyes from a doll's head, pop, pop, pop, that was the frogs, believe me, boom! A mom, her children, and a fuel truck, melting flesh, shrieks like napalm holiday streamers, it ain't the Fourth of fuckin' July, but the snap of the master's whip, pulsing red, blue, and orange lights, that's Jesus bein' nailed on the Goddamn cross like raw sewage stuck to the roof of your mouth! Yeah, so your leanin' on the fuckin' horn, blarin' somethin' real stupid like fingernails scraped across a blackened heart, bits of metal, glass, cursin' God's fuckin' name, but no one hears you, not anymore, God is absent, "Jesusfuckers!" You ain't really here, it's only a mirrored sky, yeah, it might be New Year's Day but it's the morning after like last year's bur-den, still, you think you can make a fuckin' difference, beep! Beeeeeep! Traffic's at a Goddamn standstill, still, you haven't learned, you haven't yet stopped tryin'.

◆   ◆   ◆

Jesus, I've got a mouth full of mud, blood-soaked eyes, a necklace of ears, some other guy's fuckin' blood on my chest like a war medal, nothin' but bullet holes up my sleeve, "No!" I can't see the tree line from here, it's all only noise, and noise anymore, the birds, the laughter, the kids, it all bleeds into metal scraps, frags, bits, pieces, "Yeah!" Nothin' fits like Humpty, Dumpty, together, again, my dreams are of steel, pile drivers, but I'm naked, see through like divin' backwards into pools of concrete winter, a sea of dead leaves, a convicted murderer's last meal, a workhorse with blinders, and all we eat is mud from cans, a holiday slice of black pitched sky, and the wounded dog cries out from under the plow, a tractor trailer, hazardous waste, the onslaught of traffic, back out the back of my Godforsaken brain like a dying soldier's final cry, but fuckin' God won't let him die! "Fuck you, God! Jesus hates you!" There, I've done it, and the line, the wire, strings are all balled up, pulled tight, tighter yet, and the marionette chokes, and out from this, and into Knot! Jesus, it was me who wandered off.

◆   ◆   ◆

Knots are made of blood, shreds of toilet tissue, black ink, and are held on with tape, sometimes glue, Knots exist only in gray space, are the same on all sides, but not the same, goin' sideways, without moving (no heads, tails, north, or down), no borders, fronts, but facing in all directions, taut, stretched to the limit, but! Free floating, carefree, "No!" Nothin' to go for, and goin' fuckin' nowhere! Knots are not happy, sad, pining, or numb, greater than windows, less than heaven, eternally grateful, humble, and don't know it.

◆   ◆   ◆

Knots are like abbreviated run-on sentences whose meaning escapes me.

◆   ◆   ◆

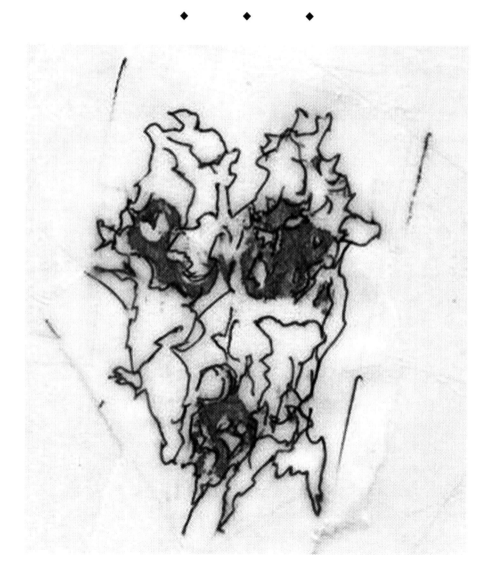

9

"Burp"

"If!" If only for these bodily functions is there any reprieve.

◆   ◆   ◆

After that last play, *Welcome Home,* I got stuck in that basement, all I wrote for the next six years was noise, forty notebooks full. Those one-hundred-sheet composition books, you know, with black-and-white Knots on the front and back cover. I'd fill both sides of the page, four lines above the first line, two lines between the lines. Six boxes full, a closet full of boxes. I couldn't complete a Goddamn fuckin' sentence, run on, and on, just runnin'. And nothin' got in, and nothin' got out. At first I was unaffected by the noise like a city dweller to traffic's snarl, but later it would consume me like the gnashing of teeth.

◆   ◆   ◆

10

"The Wall"

I don't want to be doin' this anymore. I'm sick to death of my own story, but there's only one way out. I'm up against the outer Wall, motherfucker! I'm unstoppable.

◆   ◆   ◆

I went to all kinds of meetings, Al-Anon, CoDA, Adult Children of Alcoholics, read whatever self-help books, books about trauma, the Bible, front to back, each chapter three times, even went to church on Sundays, sometimes during the week. Still, I hadn't a clue, an inkling who or what might fix me. Ann suggested a twelve-week residential program for PTSD (posttraumatic stress disorder). It was all I'd left to try, but I'd have to wait a few weeks. In the interim, James thought it might do me some good to visit the Wall, he'd even pay for the trip. I'd left my parents home a month earlier, had stopped working altogether, it was getting harder to leave my room. I'd count the cars from the trucks passin' without looking, without leaving my bed. James was HIV-positive, I thought I might be of some assistance, moved in with him up north, a country postcard kind of town with a tiny train station, a secret underground passage, and big old oak trees whose leaves were in flame. James was afraid he'd never see them leaves again. Even though we routinely shared needles I somehow missed the virus both he and Bubba caught.

I'd never been to the Wall before. It was Veterans Day 1993. I made the trip with Patrick, a sober vet I'd known from city meetings. We didn't know each other that well, but this trip would change all that. He was fuckin' nuts, had a bull's-eye tattooed on the back of his bald head, didn't want them to miss. "They just want us dead!" we told each other repeatedly, we'd served our purpose. Me too, I guess, I was fuckin' nuts. It was the year they were dedicating a statue commemorating the women who'd served in Vietnam. We drove down the day before, spent the night at a Holiday Inn.

We were both up at five, smoking cigarettes, drinking coffee, and writing in our journals. There seemed no difference between us, we were both on edge, anxious, and shared the same demons.

We got to the Wall about 7:00 A.M., no crowds yet, people were just beginning to arrive. I wore a first Cav pin, and everyone I saw with a first Cav pin or patch I'd ask what company they were with, I was desperately looking for someone I knew. "Welcome home, welcome home, welcome home" was all anyone said like I'd just arrived, come home, assuming, I ever did come back.

"If!"

"Yeah" was my only response. As the day wore on I became that much more desperate. Patrick, too. The situation only got worse, hopeless, futile, all these soldiers, and nobody I knew. Where the fuck was Myles, anyway?

Our first trip along the Wall, that longest walk, I found the names, saw the faces of ghosts, Rodney C. Brown, I ran my fingers over, over and again, over the groves, "If!" Bounce, bouncin' Betty, fuckin' B-40! Buttkins, Henderson, Walsh, Casey fuckin' Jones, but they left out the *fuckin'*. Patrick's name was on the Wall with a different middle initial. I knew what the fuck he was thinkin', "If!"

It occurred to me that other names were missing—O'Brien, Smyth, Uncle Joe, Charlie, thousands of others, hadn't their suicides been motivated by the war, hadn't the war killed them too? I had an idea, they should build an outer Wall about twenty-five yards from this existing Wall, encircling it with the names of the postwar fallen. Might there be twice, or thrice as many names? You'd have to walk the path between the Walls, from side to side and ghosts be snappin' at your heels, picking at your brain. You'd have to ask yourself why. What part did you play, or not play, how had you contributed to this tragic fuckin' mess! Again I thought, we were all wrong.

Each pass we made along the Wall, the greater the crowds, the more things left behind, boots, wineglasses, photographs, letters, children's drawings, tarnished medals, all that remained the same were the names, you couldn't change that. I kept askin', but there was no one, no one I knew had been left alive. Truly, truly I believed, Jesus, I must be the last dead soldier still breathing.

As the parade entered the grounds and began to disperse, about three hundred of us guys, all Vietnam vets, made a path for the women to pass through, wheelchairs parted, canes saluted, we were all applauding, "Thank you, thank you, thank you," I kept saying it over, over and again, I was crying, it was somethin' no one had ever said to me. One kind nurse with angelic features, back lit and haloed, broke file, came over and gave me a hug, this started Patrick cryin' too.

The unveiling of the statue was to take place later that afternoon. We kept walking around, circlin' the grounds, thousands of people doin' the same thing too, like one giant fuckin' merry-go-round. That ride always made me sick. "Welcome home, welcome home, welcome home." Shut up already! I just kept seein' the same ghostly faces, the same faded green fatigues, the same patches, ribbons, and purple hearts, over, over and again, and nobody I knew. I finially realized with sudden impact like runnin' smack damn into a Wall that I wasn't looking for someone I knew. No! But for that part of me I'd lost. And thousands of others like war trolls were doin' the same thing too, but most of 'em didn't know it. And all these POW-MIA flags, we are the prisoners, missing in action. And up against the outer Wall motherfuckers!

Simultaneously, Patrick and I turned to each other with a simple request, "Let's leave." We never did stay for the ceremonies.

◆   ◆   ◆

Later that month, at my twenty-fifth year high-school reunion, after eight years, nine months, and twenty-seven days of sobriety, I got fuckin' drunk!

◆   ◆   ◆

11

"Summation"

I've not that much more to tell. Spent six months in the VA hospital, did that twelve-week program, and another. And the flashbacks only got worse, the pink, and blue, and gray of it. I was eventually diagnosed with PTSD, awarded 100 percent disability, Jesus, it only took 'em twenty-five years to figure that one out. Still, I'd be grateful, they'd got me this computer, taught me how to use it.

I'd hell to pay getting sober again, been on and off that wagon ever since, and again, over and again. Seen only anxiety, depression, loneliness, ain't nothin' like them panic attacks. I've been in and out of programs, hospitals, jails, psych wards, therapies, groups, assorted medications. I'm only tired, and worn out anymore.

◆   ◆   ◆

I'm not really alone here, it just feels that way. I've still got metal leaking out my leg. It's wintertime. I've got a orange malignant knotlike fist in my throat, a tattered flag draped over my shoulders, this rocker doesn't really rock anymore, there's no longer any front-porch view. I'm free, freezing to death. That's it, I guess, I'm waving, and the wind chimes insistently like a child waving goodbye. I am one blue branch of sky!

My cigarette ash falls to the page.

978-0-595-41858-9
0-595-41858-9

Printed in the United States
82637LV00004B/391-429/A

9 780595 418589